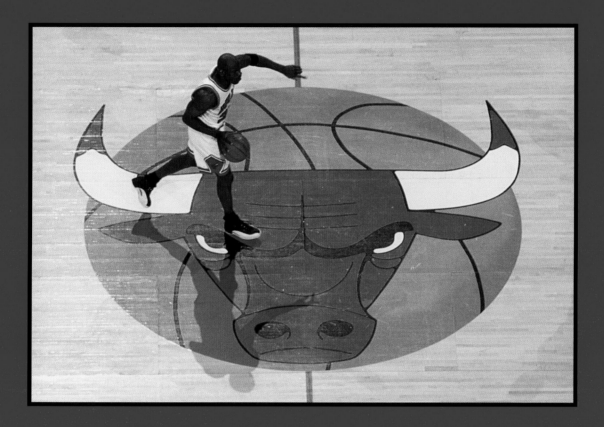

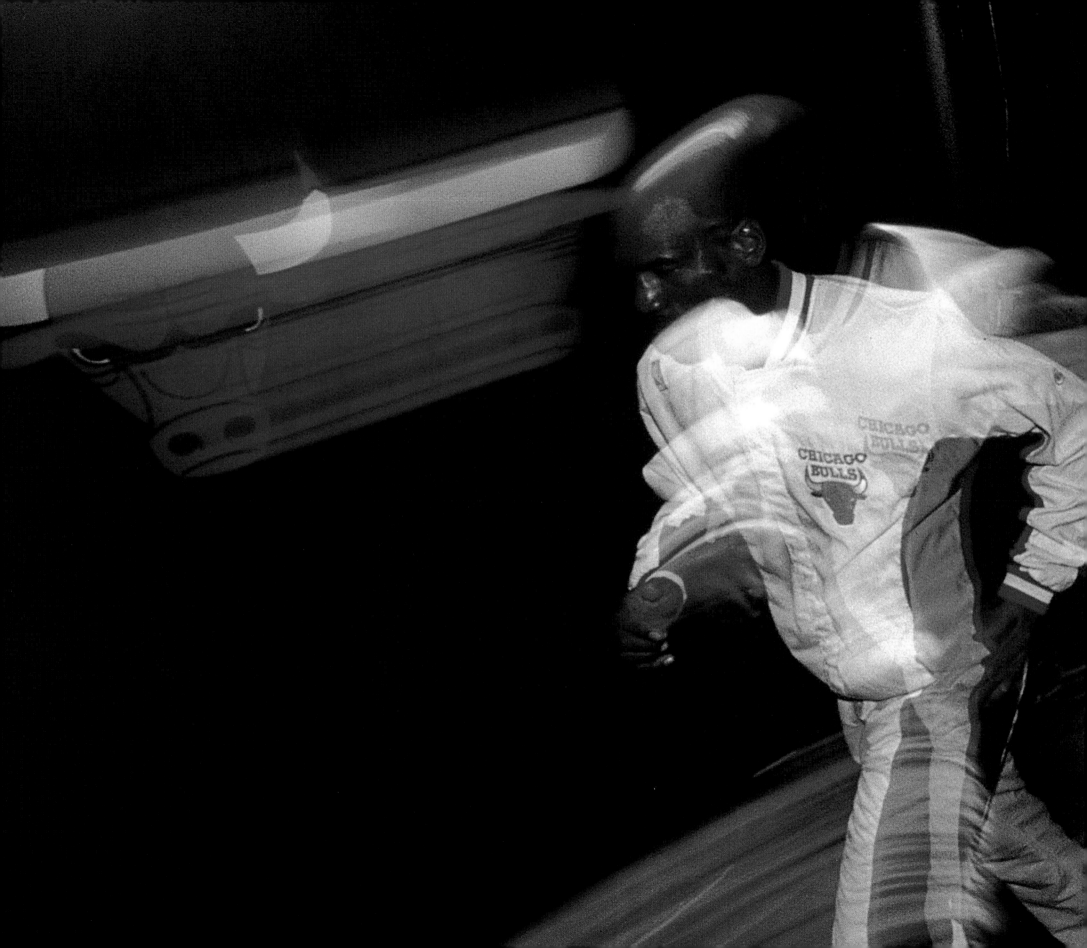

CHICAGO BULLS

THE AUTHORIZED PICTORIAL

BY ROLAND LAZENBY • PHOTOS BY BILL SMITH

THE SUMMIT PUBLISHING GROUP

One Arlington Centre, 1112 East Copeland Road, Fifth Floor

Arlington, Texas 76011

summit@dfw.net

www.summitbooks.com

Printed in Hong Kong

01 00 99 98 97   010   5 4 3 2 1

Library of Congress Cataloging-in-Publication Data

Lazenby, Roland.

Chicago Bulls : the authorized pictorial / by Roland Lazenby ; photos by Bill Smith

    p. cm.

    ISBN 1-56530-271-0 (trade paper). -- ISBN 1-56530-270-2 (hard cover)

    1. Chicago Bulls (Basketball team)--History. 2. Chicago Bulls (Basketball team)--Pictorial works. I. Smith, Bill, 1950- II. Title.

GV885.52.C45L392 1997   97-21212

                                                             CIP

Cover and book design by Dennis Davidson

Foreword

The 1996-97 Bulls season was like hiking a mountain range over small hills, valleys, and ridges, stumbling over boulders along the way. Then, against the toughest opponent ever, hoisting the flag on top of the highest peak.

It started a couple of days after we won our fourth World Championship when we signed Phil Jackson to a new one year contract, making him the highest paid coach in the NBA. It continued a few weeks later when we signed Michael Jordan to the richest single season contract in team sport's history.

The summer off-season work continued with around-the-clock negotiations that landed Dennis Rodman back in the fold for the second richest single season contract ever given to a Bulls player.

It was capped by the re-signing of veteran forward Jud Buechler and the addition of future Hall of Famer, Robert Parish, to the roster.

That was before we ever practiced or played a game in anger. The summer work done, let the fun begin. Except for Michael, Scottie and Parish, none of our players had ever been on a defending championship team and didn't know how hard it would be to repeat.

The valleys got larger in the form of injuries and weariness on bodies strained by so little time off between seasons. Scottie Pippen and Toni Kukoc played in the World Championship for the USA and Croatia and had little time to recover. Nagging injuries from the previous year didn't have enough time to heal.

Phil, Tex Winter, Jimmy Rodgers, Frank Hamblen, and Bill Cartwright conducted an easier training camp than usual, allowing players to get ready more slowly.

The medical staff of trainer Chip Schaefer, team doctor Jeff Weinberg, and orthopedists Michael Lewis and Ira Kornblatt backed by long-time strength and conditioning coach Al Vermeil and his assistant Erik Helland became more crucial than ever before as the injuries piled up.

photo by Barry Elz

Dennis, Toni, Jason Caffey, Bill Wennington, Randy Brown, Luc Longley, and Dickey Simpkins all went down. Michael and Scottie amazingly played through pain and discomfort all year.

Dennis was suspended twice, and Jason was called upon. Luc was injured in a swimming accident. Toni and Bill both had serious plantar fasciitis, enough in Bill's case to keep him off the playoff roster. Toni played in pain that kept him hobbling much of the latter part of the year.

Late in the season, because we began working on it early in the season, we were able to shock the entire league and bring in a quality player in Brian Williams. He was a key factor in our championship drive in the playoffs.

In the early playoff rounds, we played well enough to beat Washington and Atlanta without playing too many games. Miami tested us in the Eastern Finals and got us ready for our toughest opponent in five championship series, the Utah Jazz. Ex-Bull Jerry Sloan's Jazz never gave up for one second. It took one of the greatest individual performances I've ever witnessed, that of M.J. in the fifth game in Utah, to put us in a position to win.

In game six, at home, in front of the greatest fans in the world, it came down to the last few seconds and Steve Kerr hit a fifteen-foot jump shot to wrap up our fifth title.

We hoisted the trophy and the fans saw Jerry Reinsdorf, myself, the coaches and players.

The people whom the fans didn't see—my assistant Jimmy Stack, Scouts Clarence Gains and Ivica Dukan, Vice Presidents Irwin Mandel and Steve Schanwald, Karen Stack (my left arm), equipment man John Ligmanowski, the entire group behind the scenes—were just as important to the organization as those up front.

The journey was over, the flag hoisted, and we all could finally relax— for the moment.

Jerry Krause
Vice President Basketball Operations

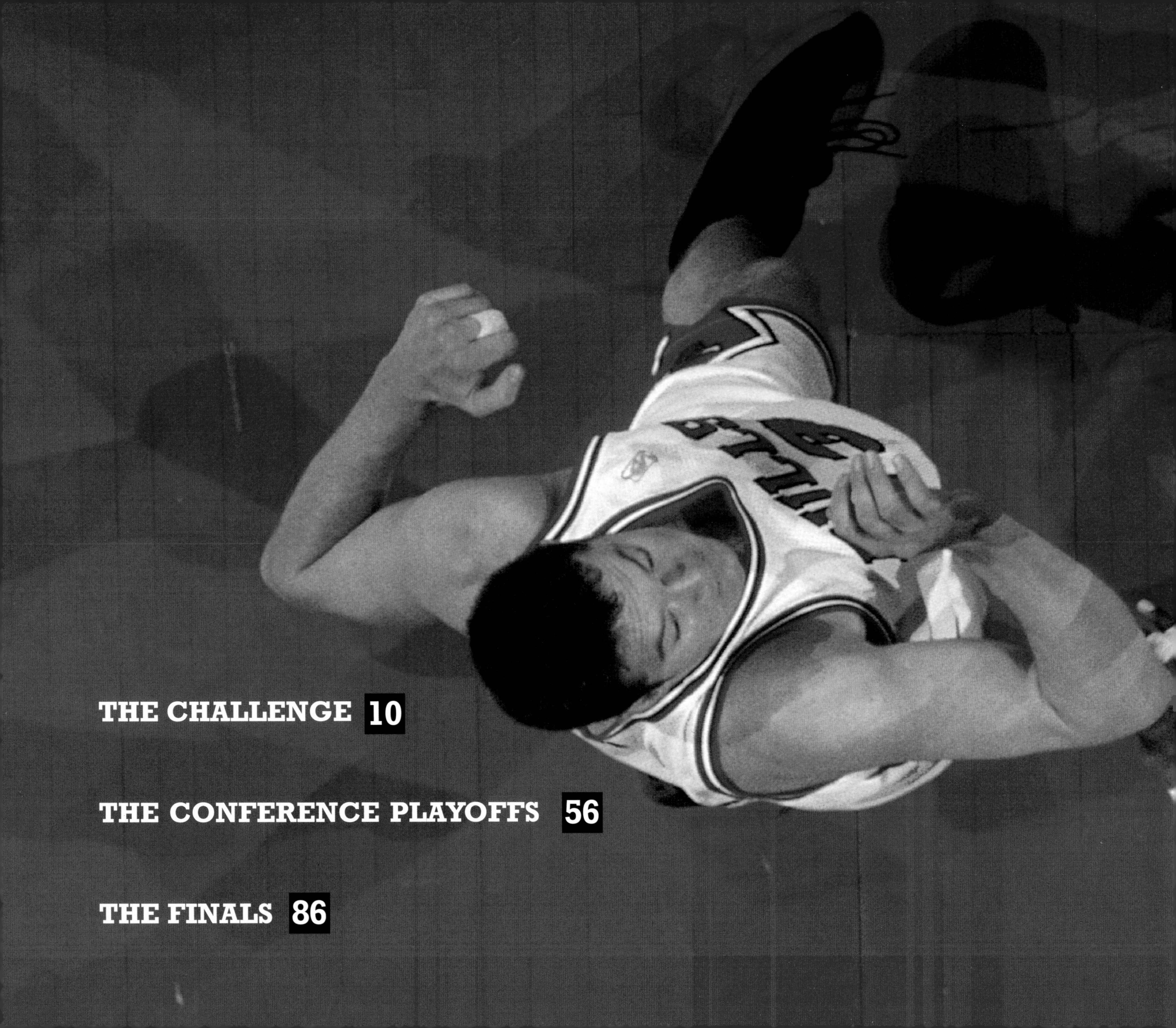

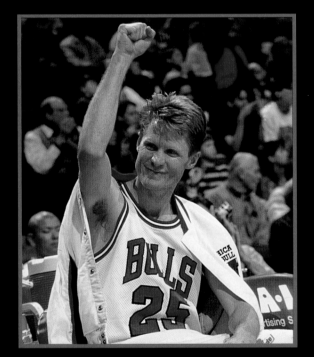

In pro basketball, there is a simple axiom: Nothing is easy the second time around. Or the third, the fourth, or the fifth, for that matter. That notion has held true since the early seasons of the National Basketball Association, when the Minneapolis Lakers and Boston Celtics gutted their way to a series of championships.

Yet the process of winning spoiled the fans for both teams, so much so that they struggled to sell tickets. The Michael Jordan-led Chicago Bulls, of course, have never had that problem. The waiting list for seats at the United Center runs twenty-one thousand deep, and the ratings jump whenever the Bulls appear on television.

Still, there is that inevitable "spoiled" atmosphere around this team. Basketball operations V.P. Jerry Krause has built a team so good that the Bulls are expected not to just win but to dominate and confuse the opposition night after night with increasingly magical performances.

All of which means that in Chicago, the encore is the supreme challenge. "What the hell are we gonna do this time around?" coach Phil Jackson always has to ask himself. That was certainly the prevailing thought heading into the 1996-97 season as the Bulls launched Phase II of their Quest for Ultimate Hoops Glory.

Phase I, you may recall, involved the 1996 campaign, which the team concluded with an all-time best 72-10 regular season record and a 15-3 playoff run that netted the Bulls their fourth championship in six seasons.

No sooner had the confetti settled to the ground from that celebration than the media—and the Bulls themselves—began trumpeting "The Drive for Five," that overwhelming assumption that the team was going to claim its fifth championship in 1997.

Once again, the greatest obstacles seemed to be the excesses of success itself, with the players accumulating so much in new business, new contracts, new product endorsements, that they hardly had time to count the money. After all, the championship series concluded in late June 1996, and the celebration finally settled down sometime in July.

Poor Dennis Rodman struggled to cram in the international shooting schedule for his movie *Double Team* and to start production of his MTV series *World Tour* before training camp opened in October. That's not to mention autograph sessions, book promotional tours, and junkets to Las Vegas that he felt compelled to undertake.

For Scottie Pippen, the business deals included his appearance on Dream Team III, the United States's basketball entry into the Summer Olympic Games in Atlanta, which he followed with surgery on a bad ankle. Guard Ron Harper and center Luc Longley also underwent off-season surgery and recuperation. No wonder the Bulls coaching staff was eager to see just how big a toll success and all its gnarly attachments had taken on the team's togetherness.

A Growing Curiosity

"We were all very curious," said assistant coach Jimmy Rodgers, "as to how our team was going to respond after we won the championship and played into June and accomplished what we accomplished last season, winning over seventy games and then having a short summer. We were all curious as to how our team would reenergize and come back."

In Rodman's case, the answer was immediate and disappointing. In the media session opening the season, he told reporters just how bored he was

by basketball, a jarring revelation in that the team had just agreed to pay him better than $9 million to play the upcoming season.

"I know Dennis made some statements in the opening press conference that he's not so excited about this," Jackson acknowledged later. "But in effect, I tried to diffuse that with the team by saying that we're fortunate that we're all back together again." Indeed, Jerry Krause had retained the core roster from the championship team, jettisoning only deep subs James Edwards and Jack Haley while adding forty-three-year-old former Celtic great Robert Parish as a reserve center.

Back were young forwards Jason Caffey and Dickey Simpkins, still charged with bringing energy off the bench; guards Randy Brown, the defensive specialist, and Steve Kerr, the three-point weapon; multifaceted Toni Kukoc with his unique passing and ballhandling skills; Bill Wennington, the reserve center who worked so effectively as a spot-up shooter; and swingman Jud Buechler, whom the coaches called from the bench whenever they wanted to inject a little mayhem into the proceedings.

Mixing these components with starters Jordan, Pippen, Longley, Harper, and Rodman provided the Bulls coaching staff with an enviable set of options. "There's not another club in the league that kept its same unit together," Jackson said. "And we have this history of being together. There's so much less that we have to work at. There's so much more that we can experience as a team because we have that memory and that knowledge of how to do it out there on the court."

Amazingly, the league had been overrun with an unprecedented rush of free agency migration that saw nearly two hundred players change teams. The reshuffling of rosters created chaos on most other teams and a tremendous window for the Bulls. "We've got the opportunity to do this again," Jackson told his players as camp began. "It's a wonderful opportunity."

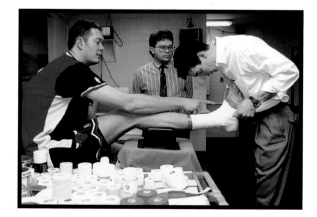

After a brief stint at their camp at the Berto Center in suburban Chicago, the Bulls opened the exhibition season with an early October weekend swing through Las Vegas to play the Seattle Super Sonics in a rematch of the 1996 NBA Finals.

Vegas seemed the perfect place for the Bulls to begin their campaign, because the season was something of a gamble for the organization, with team chairman Jerry Reinsdorf showing once again his commitment to winning another championship by agreeing to plunk down a league-record $57 million payroll to see if his club could complete that "Drive for Five."

On the court at the Thomas and Mack Center, Rodman wasted little time in making it clear just how much of a crapshoot Reinsdorf's gamble really was. He got a second technical late in the game against the Sonics and was booted, causing him to immediately rush at official Ken Maurer. Rodman snapped his head as if to butt Maurer, but teammate Randy Brown was there to pull him out of the way.

Afterward, Jordan implied that Rodman was just showing off for his Vegas fans, which may have been the case, because Rodman cooled down immediately and trotted across the court to give his jersey to a woman in a wheelchair, all to deep applause from the sellout crowd. Jordan, though, sounded a caution that Rodman's seeming indifference could be a storm gathering on the team's horizon.

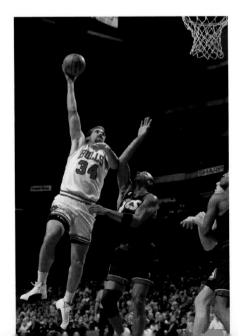

17

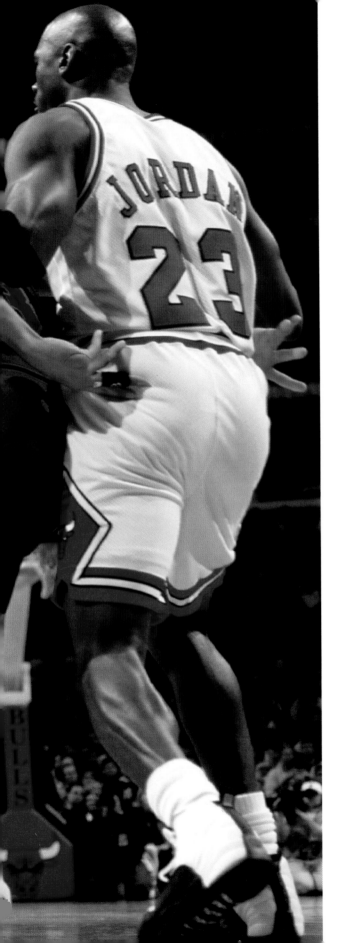

Bulls coach Phil Jackson agreed. "It will be a very different year," he said after the game, his face already weary. "I just don't know what to anticipate. I try not to anticipate. Just let it happen. Our whole scenario, our whole buildup of this ball club is that we alone can destroy our opportunities."

The other big question, Jackson acknowledged, was, "Will we be able to sustain our effort because of the age we have on our crew?" Rodman was thirty-five, Jordan would turn thirty-four during the season, and Harper and Pippen were well into their thirties. Could they withstand the grind of another championship push? What about the mental toll of meeting the challenge night after night in the eighty-two-game schedule and mustering the competitive intensity required?

"Maybe the monotony might build or the 'same-old, same-old' that happens to a ball club," Jackson said. "So we've got to keep it fresh and new as often as we can so we can make it as entertaining as last year."

The press, meanwhile, was wondering if the one-year, $30 million contract Jordan had signed with the team meant that this would be his final NBA season. They also wondered if the one-year contracts given to Rodman and Jackson would undermine the Bulls' chemistry.

"A lot of times in this modern-day game, people relax because they know they're going to be around for three or four years," Jordan said. "I think what we're showing is that we're going to play for the moment. We're gonna give our best moments, our best effort. We're not going to sit back and say, 'We've got another three or four years on our contract, maybe we can take a day, take a year off.' We're gonna come out here and play each and every game like it's our last."

Jordan on High

If there was anything about the Bulls that wasn't open to question, it was Jordan himself. There was no better proof of this than that preseason game in Las Vegas. Although it was only an exhibition, Jordan's eyes were afire, and he was going full blast in an amazingly physical battle with Craig Ehlo, who had just signed on with the Sonics. They pushed and shoved and fought so

21

hard for position that Jordan even took a quick swing at Ehlo that was missed, or ignored, by the officials.

He wanted to make it clear that he was starting off this season the way he closed things out last year. "I want to be consistent every night," Jordan explained afterward. "I want to step on the court and accept every challenge."

The Bulls whipped Boston on the road to open the regular season, then returned home to the United Center to receive their 1996 championship rings. The Bulls' jewelry was a paperweight of gold with an onyx setting, encrusted with seventy-six sweet little diamonds, one for each of the team's seventy-two wins last season, plus another four representing the franchise's four NBA titles.

The Bulls received their rings in a coronation ceremony that included taped flourishes of horns and a stroll by each player down a long red carpet out to the spotlight at center court, where they received their rings and a handshake from league commissioner David Stern. Dennis Rodman, of course, collected only the ring, ignoring the commissioner's extended hand. After that, the Bulls raised their fourth championship banner to the rafters. Once the banner was in place, Jordan and company then proceeded to destroy the Philadelphia '76ers.

Highly touted Sixers rookie Allen Iverson and his talented backcourt mate, Jerry Stackhouse, were through by the end of the third quarter, their team down by thirty points. They sat together on the floor, leaning against a press table, looking thoroughly befuddled and embarrassed while the subs played out the clock. The Bulls, of course, have a way of doing that to people, particularly spirited rookies.

From there, the Bulls rolled out to the best start in franchise history, eviscerating twelve straight opponents. Jordan gave the blastoff a little extra push by zipping Miami for fifty points in the third game of the season. The motivation for this outburst could be traced to the spring before when sportswriters

  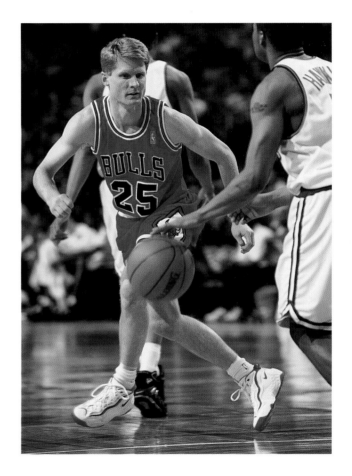

and analysts began debating whether Chicago was the greatest team ever. Individually, Bulls players were reluctant to speak out on the issue. As Jordan pointed out, "Anybody else win seventy-two games?" Yet there was little question that the Bulls saw the 1996-97 schedule as an opportunity to settle the matter once and for all.

After Philadelphia fell, Chicago defeated Vancouver, Miami, Detroit, Boston again, Phoenix, Miami again, Charlotte, Atlanta, Phoenix again, and Denver, in that order. Most of the games weren't even close.

The streak had followed the Bulls' familiar pattern of the previous season. They often toyed with a team early, then selected some point, usually in the second or third quarter, to break the opponent down with pressure defense. It was a pattern that would persist through-out the '96-97 campaign. "It's definitely satisfying to come out every night and feel like we dismantle people at some point in the game," said Chicago center Luc Longley. "We've done that every game so far and that's fun."

The sign was a certain look of defeat in opponents' eyes, usually after Jordan made a shot and gave them a smile or a wink, which talked louder than trash. "I see that almost every night," Longley said. "That's one of the great things about playing on this team." Asked about the look of defeat in the other team's eyes, Jordan replied, "Sure. You can tell."

Asked if he ever thought about pitying any of his victims, Mike quickly said, "No. No one ever pitied me when I was (in the same situation) earlier in my career. No pity. We just want to go out and keep this going."

Part of the Bulls' success rested on the fact that most teams continued to run isolation offenses against them. When it didn't work, those teams for some strange reason had no second option. "That plays right into our favor, playing half-court offense with that isolation situation," Jordan said. "I think we have enough of a team defense to collapse. If we need to double-team, we rotate well, and we have good individual defensive players. If the other team misses, we rebound the ball and start our break."

It would have been good strategy for opponents to run the Bulls and force them to shift strategy to control the tempo. But few teams could run wisely.

With the team struggling to regain its competitive nucleus, it had been Jordan who pushed things
ahead with his intensity. He was named the league's
Player of the Month for November after averaging
31.9 points, 4.9 rebounds, 3.4 assists, and 1.5 steals
while playing nearly thirty-six minutes per game.
He did this while completing the renovation of his
offensive game into the sport's deadliest jump-
shooting weapon.

A Smart Move

"Michael is relying a little bit more on the outside
shot," observed Tex Winter, the Bulls seventy-five-
year-old assistant coach and offensive guru, "but I
think that's what he feels he can get the easiest out of
the offense, that and the postup. He's not trying to
take the ball to the hole as much as he did at one
time, and I think that's wise that he doesn't. He's still
getting his thirty-plus points a ball game, and he's
getting it a little easier than he did at one time. At his
age, that's a smart thing."

On November 30, against San Antonio, Jordan
scored his twenty-five thousandth career point, making him the second fastest player in league history
(behind Wilt Chamberlain) to reach that milestone.

No sooner had talk of bettering last season's
record-breaking 72-10 season started to get serious than trouble struck. The team suffered its first
loss in a road game at Utah where Rodman was

The Dynastic Duo. Jordan with Celtic legend Bill Russell, the man who led Boston to eleven titles in thirteen years.

Jordan and Pippen walk out of the Ritz Carlton in Washington, D.C.

Future Hall of Famer Robert Parish on a return trip to Boston where he played most of his career.

Luc Longley working on his rehab in the team pool.

badly outplayed by Karl Malone and cost the Bulls the game with a crucial late technical for shoving Jeff Hornacek. Afterward, Rodman said he had been bored by the proceedings.

A few nights later, the Bulls nearly suffered a second loss to the Los Angeles Clippers when forward Loy Vaught made Rodman look bad. "If we win it again, I'll come back," Dennis said afterward, while wearing pink suede shoes and a blue suede jacket. "If we don't, I'm getting out. I've already made my mark in this game. I've got other things to do."

That same week, the pressure on Rodman increased dramatically when Bulls center Luc Longley injured his shoulder while body-surfing in California. Longley, after all, is the dinosaur in the Bulls' arsenal, the giant body who anchors their defense and plays the pivotal pinch-post position in their triangle offense. Although Longley (who would be out of action until

January) had been prone to bouts of erratic play, he had given the Bulls the frontcourt size that presented matchup problems for many other teams. Longley's absence only placed more pressure on Rodman at a time when the forward was struggling to find the focus and motivation to once again be the man in Chicago's frontcourt.

The Bulls returned home to suffer their second loss of the season, to the Miami Heat, which brought more complaints that Rodman had been outplayed by the Heat's P.J. Brown. The Heat erupted in ecstatic celebration on the United Center floor after the victory. "We'll have that memory," Jordan promised afterward.

In a loss the next night in Toronto, Jordan was clearly winded from playing better than forty minutes against the Heat the previous night. He scored just thirteen against the Raptors on five of seventeen shooting and failed to

Rodman studies more videotape than anybody in the NBA.

"Virtually every Bull has a pregame routine," Bill Smith says. "For Dennis, it's going to the team weight room. He lifts before the game, after the game, two or three times a day. He's never in the locker room. He sits in the weight room before a game, eating a take-out meal of spaghetti or chicken."

score at all in the second half. In the fourth quarter, Jordan would post up only to kick the ball out, usually to Pippen, who finished with twenty-eight.

This time Rodman couldn't keep up with Raptors forward Popeye Jones and was ejected late in the game for disputing an offensive foul call. Afterward, in a locker-room interview with Sports Channel, Rodman spewed out a profanity-laced invective against the officials and league commissioner David Stern. The Bulls responded a day later by informing Rodman after practice that he would be suspended for two games, costing him approximately $104,000 in fines (subtracted from his $9 million salary).

Jackson pointed out that Rodman had played hard in the Bulls' three losses—"He just seemed less interested. Right now Dennis is struggling to find a direction to be challenged every game," Jackson said. "I keep telling him that he's going to get that rebounding title, and things are going to go his way." As he had the previous season, Rodman came back contrite and strongly focused after his suspension. But there were more danger spots ahead.

The Bulls, meanwhile, had continued to prosper without Rodman's full attention. They racked up a 15-1 November and sank to 11-4 in December but finished the month by winning ten of eleven games.

The highlights of the first half of the season were topped by a December overtime win over the Lakers in the United Center. Los Angeles had dominated Chicago through three quarters, building a fat lead until the Bulls' pressure defense began forcing Lakers turnovers in the fourth quarter, and Toni Kukoc got hot from three-point range. His thirty-one points allowed the Bulls to tie it at the buzzer, then break it open 129-123 in overtime, leaving the young Lakers aching and embarrassed.

Jordan had thirty and Pippen thirty-five points, making it the first time in team history that three players had scored more than thirty in a single game.

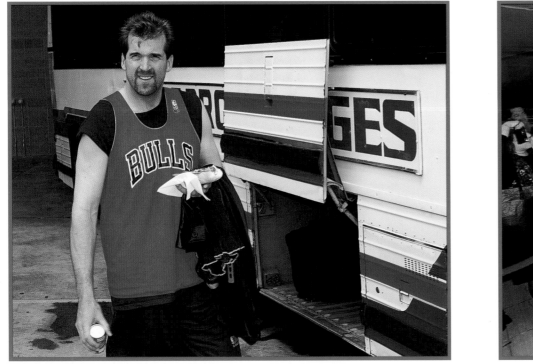

Added to the Lakers' pain was the fact that the game drew one of the largest national cable television audiences ever. They faltered before millions of witnesses. "Everyone who saw that game knows that we beat ourselves," Shaquille O'Neal said. "We couldn't get the ball past half-court. I didn't take any shots in the last twenty-five minutes because we couldn't get the ball past half-court."

No one was more burned by the turn of events than Lakers coach Del Harris, who drilled his team on beating the press at every available opportunity after that loss. His goal was to be ready for the February rematch with the Bulls in Los Angeles.

The Bulls opened 1997 by winning their first seven games, including a 110-86 thrashing of the Houston Rockets. On the 15th of January, Jordan passed Alex English (25,613) to become the eighth-leading scorer in league history.

Unfortunately, that night will be better known for Rodman's kicking a courtside cameraman in the groin in Minneapolis, a move that brought an eleven-game suspension and more than $1 million in fines and lost income. Jordan and Pippen had never hesitated to express their displeasure with Rodman's misbehavior, but the kicking incident brought a strong reaction from other teammates as well as fans. Observers resumed wondering why the Bulls would put up with all the shenanigans. The answer, however, lay in the videotape of 1996's playoff games when Rodman's masterful rebounding and forceful frontcourt play rescued Chicago night after night.

Getting the Message

"There was no question," Tex Winter said, "that the situation got to the point where it was 'one more deal and you're outta here.' But at the same time it was never addressed in those terms, yet Dennis still definitely got the message." For some, the kicking incident was simply the final sign that Rodman's

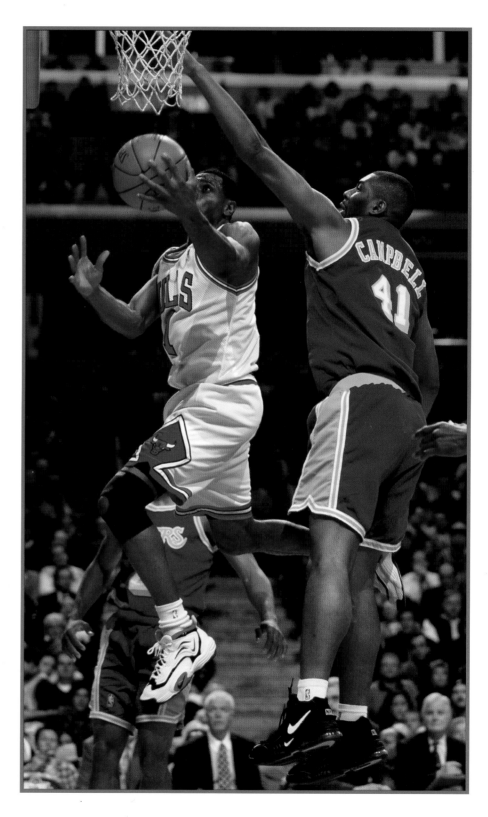

physical, emotional style of play had gone too far. "I gotta have some kind of emotion out there for me," Rodman countered. "I know the other team's not gonna do it for me, so I gotta go out there and do it myself. I try to psyche guys out. Hit 'em here and hit 'em there and try to get them out of position. Try to frustrate guys. That's my game, and it works most of the time."

Fortunately, Rodman seemed to come to his senses, realizing that he had made a terrible assumption that just about everybody admired him for his dyed hair, tattoos, body piercings, and other elements of his cross-dressing lifestyle. What many fans really appreciated were his rebounding, defense, and hard work on the basketball floor. Rodman realized in time that he had come dangerously close to losing his relationship with Chicago's fans. So he did the prudent thing. He apologized and went back to his old hard-scrambling style.

With the Rodman distraction, the Bulls suffered a 102-86 spanking in a rematch in Houston but then went on to win the last six games in January to close out the month with a 13-1 record. The run included Jordan's fifty-one points against the Knicks after New York coach Jeff Van Gundy said Jordan befriended and "conned" players on opposing teams to diffuse their competitiveness. The allegation infuriated Michael, and he answered with the kind of performance that New Yorkers have come to know all too well.

February opened with another Jordan tiff, this time with Seattle coach George Karl, who had suggested what everyone else knew, that Michael had resorted more often to jump shooting as opposed to attacking the basket. Jordan used this imagined slight to push Chicago to a 91-84 win over Seattle to open the Bulls West Coast road swing. The burst of energy propelled them to five straight wins.

Although the Lakers had lost Shaq to a January knee injury, they were fired up enough to hammer out a 106-90 win over the Bulls, who finished up the West Coast trip at 5-1 just before the All-Star break.

"When I see Michael, it just excites me," said the Lakers' Eddie Jones, who has developed into one of the game's premier defenders at two-guard. "I know he's gonna go after me. I know whoever he walks on the court against, he's definitely gonna attack that player. I'm the type of player, I always say, 'I don't want to be embarrassed on the court. I'm gonna give it my all. If I gotta pick up six fouls, I'm gonna try my best to stop him.' The only thing you can do is put a hand up. Hopefully he doesn't beat you off the dribble, hopefully he doesn't beat you with the jump shot. You just try to stay in his way at all times."

The important thing, Jones said, was never to look in his eye and never, ever engage in any conversation. "When he goes against somebody that's known as a defender, that ignites him," Jones explained. "He just wants to go out and take you out in the first quarter. He wants to show you that, 'Hey, all these people are saying that you're a defender. I want to show you how well you defend.' "

At the All-Star festivities in Cleveland, the league celebrated its fiftieth anniversary by honoring the fifty greatest players in NBA history at halftime. Jordan and Pippen were among those selected, and Jackson was picked for the list of the league's ten best coaches. To emphasize his standing,

After the team practiced at Georgetown University on a trip to Washington, the players emerged from the gym to find some kids playing outside. "All of a sudden, Scottie, Toni, and Harper started playing pickup with them," Smith said. "These kids were thrilled. The guys still had ice packs on their knees, but they played. It was basketball at its purest fun. Those kids will never forget that, the day Scottie, Toni, and Harp played 'em in pickup."

Jordan finished the game with the first triple-double in All-Star game history (fourteen points, eleven rebounds, and eleven assists). Added to Chicago's loot was Steve Kerr's win in the three-point shoot-out.

That success, plus the return of Longley and Rodman, helped push the Bulls on another big win streak coming out of the break. The stretch included a career-high forty-seven points by Scottie Pippen against Denver.

Pippen the Scorer

"Scottie all-around might be as fine a player as there is in the NBA," Winter observed at the time. "But he's not a great shooter; he's a scorer. And there's times when he's not even a great scorer. He has very poor shooting nights at times. He seems to get out of synch, out of rhythm on occasion, and it might even last over a period of several games. But he seems to always snap out of it, and the bigger the game, the better Scottie plays. If he feels like he has to, Scottie can take a lot of pressure off of Jordan, and then suddenly he becomes a real scorer, where at other times he's satisfied not to even shoot the ball. If Jordan's having a good night, and the other players are having a good night, then Pippen doesn't care about his own offense. That's one of the things that makes him a great player."

"He's had a consistent year," Jordan said of Pippen. "Last year he got off to a great start, where he was putting up some big offensive numbers. But I think you look at what he's done this year, it's been just as consistent, All-Star caliber. A lot of times he can get overlooked because of my play. But I certainly couldn't be as effective without him. We've complemented each other very well. He's certainly my MVP."

On February 22, the Bulls went to Washington and played the Bullets with President Clinton in the stands, the first time a president had attended an NBA game since the Carter administration. "He came in the locker room and greeted everybody and knew everybody's name and made it around and was comfortable talking to the team," Jackson said of the president.

Just a few days earlier, First Lady Hillary Rodham Clinton had watched the team perform in Chicago, where Rodman had presented her with his game jersey. Asked about the president's visit to the Bulls' locker room, Rodman said, "He come pointing at me and said, 'Hey, you, what are we gonna do with that jersey? We got so many nice paintings in the White House.' I said, 'Well, put it up, dammit. Put the damn thing up. Put it by you and Hillary's and your daughter's picture. That would make a good portrait.'

"I told him that me and your wife—we're kind of related a little bit," Rodman added with a laugh. "She told me when she was in Chicago, 'You know we're related.' I said, 'In more ways than one.' So we had fun with that."

On the court against Washington, Jordan struggled for three quarters, then wowed the crowd and the president with a fourth-quarter shooting display that drove Chicago to yet another victory. "It's always a matter of time with Michael," Phil Jackson said with a smile. "He has that incredible energy level, and you know there's a point in the game where he'll just take it over and destroy a team."

It all translated into those same old feelings of invincibility, Jackson added. "We think we're doing things right, rolling along and taking care of

The Bulls' use of private jets meant that the team could come and go on airport tarmacs without having to work their way through busy terminals.

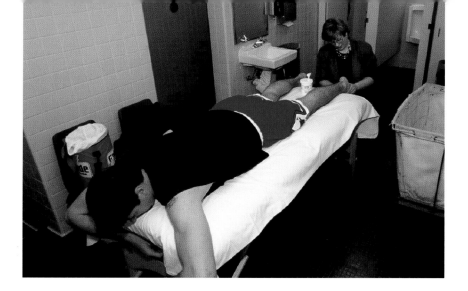

business on the road, then going home to the United Center and playing the way we want to play, maintaining that home-court attitude that we've had. Games are a little tighter, teams are playing us three and four times in the conference, and as they get to know us, they're stepping up their competitiveness."

Injuries Strike

After a 10-2 record in February, March brought its own sort of madness for the Bulls, beginning with Kukoc's foot injury and closing with a knee injury that caused Rodman to miss the remainder of the regular season. In between, the team still managed to roll up a 12-2 record, relying on the emergence of reserve forward Jason Caffey and the usual brilliance of Pippen and Jordan.

"It did a great deal for my confidence," Caffey, in his second season, said of the opportunity to play as a starter. "It was a time for me to find myself and kind of get out there and do some of the things that I can do and show people that I can play on this team and on this level. It's not an easy thing at all fitting into a team like this."

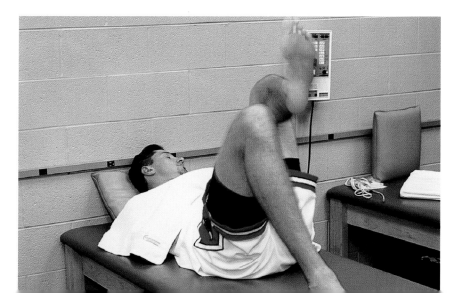

Jordan still possessed his trademark intensity, and the season had brought a new round of irritations, but it was hard for Michael to suppress his smile. "I'm having a great time," he said, "more so than last year even, because it's not the same pressure. Last year I had to prove myself. People didn't feel I could come back. I had a whole different motivation. This year I'm more relaxed. The team is more relaxed, yet we're being just as productive."

Even in the spring, after opponents had had the time to adjust their team chemistries, they still found the Bulls to be an unsolvable puzzle, rolling across April to what appeared to be a seventy-win finish.

Part of the Bulls momentum was inspired by Jerry Krause's late-season acquisition of free-agent center Brian Williams, who gave them a solid post presence. But in the homestretch, they lost three of their last four games, including a final meeting at the United Center with the Knicks. Even so, at 69-13, they tied for the second best total in league history, matching the 1972 Lakers, and they were five games ahead of the nearest competitor, claiming home-court advantage throughout the playoffs.

"We want to meet every challenge," Jordan had said at the start of the campaign.

Once again, they had done it in laudable fashion, building hope along the way that the encore would be every bit as good as the original. For that to happen, Rodman and Kukoc would have to recover from injuries and push themselves into peak playing form as the playoffs unfolded.

The city of Chicago was alive with expectations as the regular season ended. Yes, the circumstances were challenging, but wasn't that what Michael Jordan always relished, a challenge? The stage was set for what could be one of the grandest performances of all.

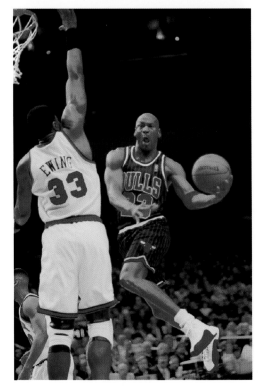

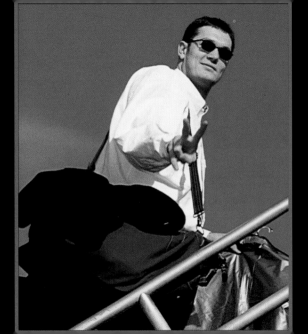

There was a funk hanging over the club. Pressing to win seventy, the Bulls instead lost three of their last four regular-season games and looked like anything but a team poised to win a championship.

Phil Jackson figured the Bulls lacked "togetherness." Their usually excellent chemistry had finally gone afoul after struggling through an injury-riddled season. To attack this problem, Jackson decided to address it with the film clips he spliced into the team's video scouting reports on the postseason. It was a traditional ploy for Jackson. Each playoff season he liked to break the monotony of the team's film sessions by splicing in nonbasketball material, which he would use to stress a basketball message.

In 1996, he had used the film *Pulp Fiction*—about hired assassins—because he wanted to boost the Bulls' killer instinct. This time around, he chose *What About Bob*, starring Bill Murray as a wacko mental patient who tried to move in with his psychiatrist.

Reserve center Bill Wennington dons a mascot outfit to give his teammates a laugh.

"Every time he used game clips, he'd put in pieces of the movie," Wennington, who missed the playoffs with a foot injury, said of Jackson. "Basically we saw the whole movie. He was implying that we got to come together, that we got to use baby steps to move along and start playing well. In the end, if we stick together and work together as a team, we're not gonna be crazy. We'll accomplish our goal, and things will work out."

Tex Winter, who sort of plays Merlin to Jackson's Arthur, says he likes to call Phil "Cecil B. DeMille." To help emphasize his basketball messages, Jackson also included clips of old *Three Stooges* movies. "It's hard for me sometimes to read exactly what the message is in Phil's movies," Winter said with a grin. "On the *Three Stooges* it was pretty easy because it was after a dumb play by one of our players."

"He's trying to break some of the monotony of going over play after play after play," center Brian Williams said of Jackson's approach. "The film always magnifies your mistakes. The film is not flattering. A lot of the times, the *Three Stooges* is appropriate because we look like the Three Stooges out there." "Tex Winter likes to sing a song when we get together for our morning sessions," Wennington explained. "He likes to sing, 'It's time we get together, together, together. It's time we get together, together again.' That song is played once in the *Three Stooges* when Moe swallows a harmonica, and they're playing him like a harmonica. They're playing that song. That's part of the message. We need to stay together as a team."

That, of course, was to become one of Jackson's main themes through the playoffs, because togetherness is a special quality in basketball, one not easily achieved, especially for the Bulls in the spring of 1997. It was a time when the separate agendas of all the players began tugging at the fabric of the team. Another factor eating at this togetherness was the question about the future hanging over the heads of Jordan, Jackson, and Rodman, all on one-year contracts. Would they be back with the Bulls for another season? There was gigantic speculation on this issue in the Chicago press.

Phil Jackson leaving practice on the motorcycle given to him by Rodman and signed by all the players.

Phil Jackson never wears his championship ring until the playoffs each year. Then he dons one as a reminder to his players.

"I think the team is a little different this year," Wennington observed in late April. "We're not as loose and relaxed as last year. We've been struggling a little bit. Things haven't been going as easy. There's a little edge on everyone. We're a little more serious. The last few weeks of the season, we weren't playing as well. We had all the injuries. They throw your rhythm off and at times make people a little testy."

Jordan, Pippen, and Harper were solid as a core. The three lifted weights together early each morning in what they called their "Breakfast Club." Rodman, of course, was an entity to himself. So was Kukoc, who is from Croatia and isolated somewhat by culture. Simpkins and Caffey and Brown shared some off-court time, and then there was the Arizona contingency of Buechler and Kerr, joined at times by Longley, the Australian, and Wennington, the Canadian. Parish and Williams were the added new elements.

Despite the potential conflicts of their success, the Bulls got along far better than the average NBA team. But winning another championship would require more than a "better-than-average" approach. It would require a supreme chemistry. Jackson, of course, was very good at pulling all the disparate elements together.

Perhaps there was no better example of this than Krause's late-season signee, Brian Williams. He, too, was a free agent, but salary-cap restrictions and league compensation rules virtually assured that he would have to move on to another team at the end of the season. Never one to show a fondness for coaches (he had played for four different teams in his six-year career), he had nonetheless fit right in with the coaching staff.

The Playoffs Begin

The eighth-seeded Washington Bullets gladly stepped up as the Bulls first-round opponent as the Eastern Conference playoffs opened in the United

Although he was only with the team a few brief weeks, Brian Williams delighted in being a Bull.

Center on April 25. The Bullets featured a dangerous starting five, led by point guard Rod Strickland, who seemed to penetrate at will and was, as Tex Winter said, "perhaps the best in the league at running the fast break."

The Bullets had a pair of excellent young forwards in Chris Webber and Juwan Howard and a mountain of a center in 7-7 Gheorghe Muresan. Calbert Cheany, the off-guard, was a fine defender just coming into his own as an offensive player, and the main threat off the Bullets' bench was three-point specialist Tracy Murray. Winter noted that although their depth was thin and their playoff experience almost nil, the Bullets had the energy and talent to be troublesome.

In the warm-up before Game 1 of the series, Muresan worked intently with assistant coach Clifford Ray, a former Bulls center from the 1970s. As he ran through shooting drills with Muresan, Ray's 1975 championship ring sparkled in the arena light, an irony lost on the '90s version of the Bulls. Ray had anchored several strong fifty-win Chicago teams in the post until 1974, when the Bulls, who had long pined for a "dominant" center, traded him to the Golden State Warriors for Nate Thurmond.

The terrible irony, of course, was that Thurmond never quite got in synch in his season in Chicago, while Ray moved into the Warriors' frontcourt and helped them immensely in their drive to the 1975 title.

The worst part of the irony is that Ray's Warriors defeated the Bulls in the 1975 Western Conference finals after trailing three games to two. Now, Ray was back for his first playoff series since helping to dash Chicago's dreams two decades earlier, and he was trying to steady Washington's young players over the giddiness of their first postseason appearance. Yet all of Ray's cautioning couldn't prevent the Bullets from giving up twenty offensive rebounds in Game 1, good enough to rescue the Bulls from their 38 percent shooting. Jordan scored twenty-eight while Pippen pitched in sixteen with ten rebounds. Off the bench, Steve Kerr contributed thirteen, including a string of three-pointers in transition that killed the Bullets just as they pulled close. The surprise factor for Chicago was Williams's eight points in the post, including two on a slick pick-and-roll with Jordan.

It all added up to a 98-86 breeze for the Bulls. About the only negative factor for Chicago was the rustiness of Kukoc and Rodman in their first game back from injury. Kukoc hit just one of ten from the field, and while Rodman had nine rebounds, he struggled and ran afoul of the refs, a pattern that would come to all but paralyze him through much of the postseason.

In the first half of Game 1, he was hit with a technical for fussing with the officials, then retreated to the bench where he got fussed at by both Jackson and Pippen. In the second half, just as Chicago had pushed to an 80-68 lead, he received his second technical and automatic ejection. Playing to the

crowd, Rodman clapped his hands along with the fans and ran to the end of the floor where official Steve Javie stood.

"As aloof as Dennis is off the court, when he steps between the lines you see what he gives you," observed Brian Williams. "You can't even look at the referees on a day like this. Either they've been told, or they've decided that they're going to stick it to him regardless. Would any other player get a T for the things Dennis said tonight? At one point he asked (official) Ted Bernhardt, 'Just watch when he's pushing me.' And he T'd him. It's obvious that Dennis cannot talk, look, or be bothered in any way with the referees. They're gonna test Dennis. He's gonna have to adapt because I doubt they will. Tonight is probably gonna be status quo."

Helping the Team

If nothing else, Game 2 made it clear that when the Bulls weren't toying with the young Bullets, the Chicago game operations crew would pick up the slack. When Washington's players came out for pregame layups, they were greeted with Frank Sinatra's "High Hopes" on the arena loudspeaker, followed up by a few riffs of the theme music for *Mission Impossible*.

Tired of that foolishness, the music director shifted to "The Time Has Come Today" for the Bulls' entrance, then the hard drivin' "Ya'll Ready for Dis?" The Bullets knew it was a legitimate question. In the layup line, Chris Webber took a deep breath, puffed up his cheeks, and let the air out slowly. Gut-check time. Then Washington came out strong and caught all of the Bulls, except for Jordan, blinking. The young Bullets hustled for loose balls, took rebounds off the board, and bodied the Bulls out of their offense.

Chicago's only answer, as had often been the case over the season, was Jordan, who proceeded through the evening like he was conducting a shooting drill in solitude. Jumper after jumper after bank shot after dunk after jumper. He made them from all over the floor while his teammates seemed to stand transfixed.

When Washington's Strickland hit a reverse at the buzzer ending the half, he pushed the Bullets' lead to 65-58. Jordan, meanwhile, finished the first two periods with twenty-six points and a face full of anger. "Michael was pretty upset at the half, and Phil wasn't real thrilled either," Steve Kerr conceded. "But there weren't many .adjustments other than attitude adjustments. Michael just raised his voice a little bit and said we had to play better."

Four minutes into the second half, the Bulls still trailed by seven, but that's when Jordan propelled them on a 16-2 run that pushed the crowd out of a slumber into outbursts of noise and energy that in turn nudged the Bulls' defensive intensity higher. The trapping defensive assault was a group effort, but on offense Jordan worked almost alone, jabbing jumper after jumper after jumper in the Bullets' faces. During time-outs, he sat motionless, a towel draped over his shoulders, head bowed, trying to conserve energy for the slaughter.

With five minutes left in the game, Jordan drove and scored, pushing Chicago up by three. Moments later, he got the ball back, motored into the lane, and flexed a pump fake that sent the entire defense flying like some third-world air force. As they settled back to earth, he stuck yet another jumper and followed it on the next possession with a drive that ended in a falling-down, impossible shot from the right baseline that pushed the lead to seven and his point total for the evening to forty-nine.

Unshaken, the Bullets cut it to 103-100 with about a minute to go. Jordan's answer was another jumper and a bank shot, the latter coming with thirty-four seconds left and driving the lead to 107-102.

Sound of Victory

Immediately, the game crew punched into the sound system that sweet little hip-hop ditty, "Whoomp, There It Is," which has come to serve as a victory cigar of sorts in Chicago in recent seasons.

During the ensuing time-out, Bulls assistant Jimmy Rodgers walked over and plucked a piece of large lint off the monk-like Jordan's ear. Michael then wrapped up a fifty-five-point night (the eighth time in his career that Jordan had scored better than fifty in a playoff game) with two free throws that provided Chicago with a 109-104 win and a 2-0 series lead.

In his postgame press conference, Jordan smiled and apologized to Tex Winter for ignoring the triangle offense and feasting on an individual scoring binge. Winter's famed triangle offense calls for the ball to be sent in to the post man, who then explores the options provided by a series of cutting teammates.

However, when Jordan takes over, the ball simply doesn't go into the post for that exploration. When Jordan goes on one of his famous scoring surges, he takes the ball right at the defense, and the challenge for the other Bulls becomes arranging their positioning or "spacing" so that double-teaming His Royal Airness won't be so easy.

Luc Longley said Jordan's conditioning alone was astounding in that it allowed him to score and play intensely active defense for more than forty-four minutes. "These are the games where he demonstrates who he really is," the center added.

"Those performances you definitely marvel at. What I marvel at is how many of them you see a year. Perhaps he only had three or four fifty-point games this year, but the thirty- and forty-point games he has almost every night. The fact that at his age he can come out physically and do the things he does every night, that's what really makes me marvel."

Yet Jordan's doing so well inevitably led to conclusions that he only did so because the rest of the team was struggling miserably. "We're out of rhythm right now," Steve Kerr admitted, "and we don't have much flow to our offense. That affects other areas of our game. Our rebound positioning is off. We got people out of position. Our defensive transition is off. We're just all out of whack." Perhaps no one was more out of whack than Rodman, who played thirteen minutes the first half and had one rebound. At halftime, Rodman changed knee braces, opting for a less cumbersome model, and found his way to seven rebounds in the second half.

"That's when we're at our best, when Dennis is clicking and rebounding and hustling inside," Longley said. "That's when we look like the Bulls that we want to be."

But for the second straight game, Rodman was called for a technical foul. "It looked like they were falling all over themselves out there to see who could call a technical on him first," Jackson said of the officials. "As a consequence, the mood kind of soured with him on the floor, and we had to get him off. Dennis is still recovering. This is a guy who suffered a serious injury. He's been under some stress physically. He hasn't been able to run, and his lateral movement is still somewhat hampered. We anticipate he's going to get better as the weeks go on and he heals."

Outside the Bulls' locker room, Jordan's agent David Falk and team chairman Jerry Reinsdorf were chatting amicably. It was the kind of day to make the lions lie down with the lambs. "I've been watching him for what is it—twelve, thirteen years? And he showed me moves I've never seen before," Reinsdorf said of Jordan. "Bill Russell once asked me what was the greatest thing about Michael, and I said it was his determination. Russell said, no, it was his imagination. He certainly had imagination tonight."

Reinsdorf was asked if Jordan's big night was a perfect dividend on the $30 million, one-year contract the team had given him. "He's earned it," the chairman said. "I've never had any regrets." Was it a good time to start contract negotiations for next year? a reporter asked. "No, no," Reinsdorf protested with a laugh.

The best-of-five series then shifted to Washington's USAir Arena, which was scheduled for closing at the end of the season. The Bullets vowed that they planned to delay that closing by extending the series, but the team's staff showed a supreme lack of faith by dressing in tuxedos to commemorate that very night as the last at the old barn. To mark the occasion, the two teams colluded in a contest of runs and dramatic reverses in fortune. The Bullets lashed out to a 14-2 start, then watched the Bulls recover to take a slim lead at the end of the first quarter. Chicago kept a two-point edge at the half, but the Bullets tied it, then ran away to take a 90-81 lead late in the fourth. The young team's mistake was taking a breath of relief with about two minutes left, which the Bulls used to rush back. They cut the lead to one with 1:12 left and closed out the series when Jordan's shot was deflected to Pippen, who grabbed the ball, went baseline, and slammed it home in the game's last seconds to put the champions up 96-95. He was fouled in the process and missed the free throw, but all Washington had left was a failed desperation shot.

The most excellent news for the Bulls was the reappearance of both Rodman (fourteen points, ten rebounds) and Kukoc (sixteen points, five

rebounds). Sensing a series loss, the Bullets staff had air guns ready to fire off confetti as the teams rushed off the floor, a strange way to greet a defeat.

Longley led the rush of Bulls through the exit tunnel toward the locker room to slap five with the team's staff members waiting there. Bringing up the rear of the group was a shirtless Rodman, who faked tossing his jersey to the clamoring fans around the exit tunnel, then smiled, and kept running into the locker room. This one, it seemed, was a keeper.

Next in Line

The Atlanta Hawks stepped up as the Bulls' next hurdle in the Eastern Conference playoffs, and, like the Bullets, they featured an excellent point guard. The Hawks' Mookie Blaylock didn't offer the same dribble penetration threat that Washington's Rod Strickland presented. Instead, he would school Chicago in his own special brand of the screen-and-roll.

"Blaylock is very nifty," fretted Tex Winter as the series was about to open. Just how nifty was obvious from the very first moments of Game 1. The Hawks pushed out to a 50-39 lead at the half, then extended it to sixteen points early in the third. The Bulls, as usual, were waiting to crack the case with their defense, which they did with a 28-12 run over an eight-minute stretch of the third period, despite yet another Rodman ejection. Then Chicago actually extended the lead to 77-70 going into the fourth, only to see the Hawks fight back. With the score tied at 97 with 2:35 remaining, Pippen stepped up with a big play, the kind of thing he had begun to do on a regular basis. In this case, he nailed a three, giving the Bulls a 100-97 lead. It says something about the defense that neither team scored from that point on.

Two nights later, in Game 2, the Bulls again presented Atlanta with the same chance for an upset, and the Hawks weren't about to let it slip by twice. Blaylock ran the pick-and-roll to perfection, and each time the

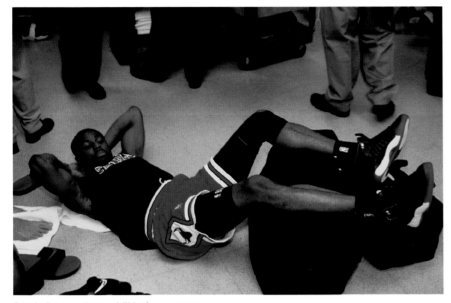

Randy Brown tries to chill before a game.

Bulls assistant coach Bill Cartwright took Longley under his wing; they became quite close over the course of the season.

Bulls hesitated to step up and defend, he dropped in a three, finishing the night with eight of them, more than enough to push the Hawks to a 103-95 win.

"We stayed aggressive," Blaylock said in his postgame assessment. "We were going to the basket. The other night we got timid and stopped looking at the basket." Asked about the Bulls' trouble with the screen-and-roll, the Atlanta point guard said, "They're really not handling it well. They're leaving me open and giving me wide-open looks."

For the first time in their incredible two-year run, the Bulls had surrendered home-court advantage in the playoffs. In fact, Atlanta became the first visiting team in two years to win a playoff game at the United Center. Chicago had won thirty-nine games against only two regular-season losses on their home floor over each of the past two years. During that same period, the Bulls had been 13-0 in home playoff games.

Now, however, the Bulls were facing back-to-back weekend games in Atlanta, leaving Pippen to warn that "unless we do the things we did all season to get sixty-nine wins, we're not going to pull another win out of this series."

"We've been living on the edge the last four games, and this time we got stung," Jordan told reporters. "But that doesn't mean we can't turn this around. I'm not ready to push the panic button yet. I'd advise you guys not to do that either."

Yet it was obvious to even the most casual observer that the Bulls were not playing well, and they seemed divided and far from the togetherness that Jackson was urging. Pippen, in particular, seemed perturbed with Rodman, who had five rebounds and six fouls in twenty-six minutes of play, plus yet another technical. "We've got to have a big effort from Dennis," Pippen said in his postgame press conference. "He's got to avoid the technical fouls. He's just got to play the game. There's a lot of other things that

During the playoffs, Rodman had a chance encounter with league officiating director Darrel Garretson. Rodman tried to pull his hat over his eyes and walk by, but Garretson stopped him for a chat, Smith recalled. "Garretson assured Dennis that the officials were not out to get him. Dennis was like a little kid trying to sneak by the teacher. I was walking with him and he saw Garretson and said, 'Oh, no!' "

Jordan had an eye for the greens in Miami and played forty-something holes before Game 4 of the conference finals. "He looked up at me as I was taking the shot and said, 'Get out of the way, Bill Smith,' " Smith recalled with a laugh. "He just wanted to go."

Dennis can do on the court. If he's not going to lead us in rebounding, don't lead us in technical fouls, because we don't need those."

Jackson later addressed the comments in a team meeting, reminding his players to stick together. "It's very unusual for this team," Tex Winter said of Pippen's open criticism of Rodman. "Generally they've been very supportive of each other. Phil handles this by saying simply, 'We're not pointing fingers at each other. Let's go out and do our jobs.' "

The other concern for the coaches was that Jordan, who had hit just twelve of twenty-nine from the floor in Game 2, suddenly seemed to be pressing on offense, as if he felt he had to carry the entire load. That, too, was addressed by Jackson, Winter later revealed. "Michael has not shot well," the veteran assistant said. "He has not shot well the whole series. The fact that he's gonna take twenty-five or twenty-seven shots, and he's not shooting well, then that puts quite a burden on your offense. If he's not shooting any better per-

centage shots than that, then he shouldn't be taking so many of them. Phil's told him not to force things, not to try to do too much, to move the ball. And Michael knows that. Michael's a smart player. But he's so competitive, and he's got so much confidence in himself that it's hard for him to restrain. I've never been associated with a player who has any less inhibitions than he does."

It was pointed out that Winter was taking the diplomatic way of saying Michael had no conscience. "Well, that's one of the reasons he's a great player," Winter replied. "He has no conscience."

Yet Jordan clearly had a sense of team and a sense of propriety. With little or no complaint, he complied with Jackson's request to ease up on his aggressiveness. Rodman's situation, however, worsened for Game 3. Suffering from a stomach virus, he didn't start and played just seven minutes and was whistled for three quick fouls, prompting Jackson to tell him at the half that the officials probably were intent on not allowing him to play.

Fortunately, Jason Caffey had stepped back into the lineup and responded with ten points and eleven rebounds to help drive the Bulls. "They had (Dikembe) Mutombo guarding me, and he was running around all day trying to block shots, and I was getting a lot of free runs to the basket," Caffey explained afterward. The Hawks, though, still zipped out to a 52-46 halftime lead as both Jordan and Pippen struggled offensively. It was the bench, specifically Kukoc (sixteen points, four rebounds, five assists) and Brian Williams (fourteen points, five rebounds), who boosted the Bulls' surge down the stretch. Both subs scored ten points in the critical fourth quarter as Chicago blew away Atlanta, 100-80, to regain the advantage in the series 2-1.

Teamed with Kerr, Caffey, and Buechler, Kukoc and Williams helped key a defensive run that held Atlanta to a franchise-low twenty-eight points in the second half. Kukoc spurred the onslaught with a pair of killer threes that zapped any hope of a Hawks comeback. "Mike had a mediocre game, but it's good for our team when he doesn't have to take too big a load, and we can get contributions from all the guys," Pippen said. "Toni has been unpredictable, but he was deadly when we needed him."

Having secured the outcome with their run, the subs came off the floor feeling like they had made up for lackluster play that had hurt in Game 2. "It was great," Kerr said, "especially after the other night when the bench was very responsible for that loss. We felt responsible when they went on a 10-1 run to open the fourth quarter and really took control of the game. So it was sort of the reverse tonight. It was nice retribution."

The other major factor was switching Harper to cover Blaylock. The Atlanta point guard scored just ten points. "We can't expect Michael to chase Mookie around for forty minutes and still be able to play offensively," Kerr said. "Harp's offensive load isn't nearly as much as Michael's. He can expend more energy. He's got the long arms. He can get his hands up in Mookie's face for the threes." "We changed philosophy on him a little bit," Winter said of the switch that helped shove Atlanta out of the pick-and-roll. "We wanted to force him to the baseline and not let him come off those picks like he did in the first two games. We put Ron Harper on him, threw a little wrinkle at him, and it helped quite a bit."

Actually, using Harper as the main defensive stopper was a ploy that had worked for much of the 1996 playoffs. But Jackson had held off on putting Harper into that role until the series moved to Atlanta, Winter explained. "Phil was kind of holding it back in reserve, waiting for the right time. Ron, he's a real pro. He's the kind of guy who's not gonna take too many shots. He's gonna look awful bad on some of 'em, but at the same time, he's apt to hit the big ones. That's one of the things that hurts teams against us. I think they're inclined to say, 'This guy can't shoot,' because really he can't. But he does."

For his part, Harper, who had been brought in by General Manager Jerry Krause in 1994, shrugged off the switch. "We've had problems guarding that size guard all season long," he said. "So we thought we had to do a job."

The Finger Routine

The Hawks' sense of being embarrassed had actually emerged in the first quarter of Game 3 when Mutombo blocked a Williams shot and turned to the crowd to wave his finger for his "not in my house" routine, while unbeknownst behind his back, Pippen was slamming in the loose ball. It was not the kind of thing one did in an NBA playoff game, and it was the first real suggestion that the Hawks might not be able to elevate their intensity to match the Bulls as the series progressed. That certainly became the case in Game 4, played the very next day in the Omni, as the Bulls opened a fat lead with a broadside of Pippen three-pointers, and the Hawks looked like people lost in traffic. When the lead stretched to twenty-four late in the game, the Chicago guys even allowed themselves the luxury of a giggle. "Some of them were down there laughing," Hawks coach Lenny Wilkens alleged, "and that will always get you fired up."

The Bulls were up 75-53 at the opening of the fourth period, but Atlanta fought back with a 27-8 run and actually cut the lead to three with about a minute left.

But the Bulls hit four free throws at the end to stay out of reach and took a 3-1 series edge with an 89-80 win.

Just two days before, the team togetherness had appeared in shreds, but it was amazing what two wins could do for unity. "I think it's pretty strong right now," Jordan said when asked about the cohesion. "We've been in a bad little slump over the past week and a half, illustrating that lack of togetherness on the basketball court. But I think over the last couple of games, we've had it. And I think that's a great beginning in terms of what we have to face going deeper into the playoffs."

The key, Jordan added, was to "make sure we're operating on all cylinders and not just one or two. We've survived, yes, but we won't survive longer if we don't get everybody involved and find the rhythm with which we're accustomed to playing. From my standpoint, I've just been trying to get everybody involved and be passive, rebound the ball, conserve energy, and let other players step up and carry that load. I just want to make sure that if I'm asked to carry an extra load in the final minutes that I'm on all cylinders and feel good in terms of energy. It's not that I don't feel I can do it consistently over the course of a whole game. I hope I'm not asked to. I think we're a better basketball team when I'm not asked to."

The difficult part of the story for Chicago again was Rodman, who played just eleven minutes and was whistled for four personals and a technical while registering just one rebound. "He's getting some tough calls called against him," Jordan said, "and in some respects that's hurting our team. Phil has tried to monitor that to where it doesn't break the rhythm of the team. Phil has done a good job of that. And Dennis has been very patient and understanding in that situation. He could have totally blown up

and done some things that would disrupt the chemistry of this team. He's hung in there, even though he knows he's getting some tough calls. He knows he put himself in that predicament."

Erasing the Doubts

The Bulls had come to Atlanta full of doubt only to exorcise it in two short days. "Obviously we haven't played good basketball over the past month," Pippen said. "When you start losing games at home it does put doubt in your mind. We realize that we're a good road team. We came in here with a mission to win both games." His smile in the postgame press conference was tinged with relief. Up 3-1 in the series, the Bulls knew they could return to the United Center and rely on the help of their crowd to close things out.

At the height of his popularity, Rodman was a deciding factor in igniting the United Center fans, who would often applaud lustily whenever he entered or left the game. If there was any immediate measure of his decline, it certainly came upon his first substitution into Game 5 on May 13 at the United Center. The usually friendly, supportive crowd offered only a smattering of applause. His response was a show of his old flair. He scored seven quick points to take the Bulls to a 33-27 lead and went on to finish the contest with twelve points (including a pair of three-pointers), nine rebounds, three assists, and a steal. He even blocked one of Mutombo's shots.

Yes, he was ejected after a profanity-laced exchange with the Atlanta center in the fourth period, but by then he had provided the inspiration his team needed to subdue the Hawks, 107-92, and claim the series 4-1. It was a grand way to celebrate his thirty-sixth birthday, and the crowd soon awakened to the presence of the old Dennis.

Jordan himself even got into the spirit, drawing a technical for wagging his finger at Mutombo after dunking on the Atlanta center just three minutes into the game. The victory sent the Bulls to their seventh appearance in the

Eastern Conference finals in nine seasons, the only problem being that they had to wait to learn the identity of their opponent. The New York Knicks had held a 3-1 series lead over the Miami Heat in the other Eastern Conference bracket, but their momentum came untracked when an overheated scuffle resulted in the suspension of a host of New York players including Patrick Ewing, John Starks, and Larry Johnson. The weakened Knicks then watched as Miami regained steam and eliminated them in the seventh game of the series.

Abruptly, the circumstances had changed. Instead of their old foes the Knicks, the Bulls now had to face Pat Riley's surprising Heat club. It was a disappointment to the Chicago fans, not to mention network executives keen on TV ratings. But there was little doubt that meeting Riley still struck a match to Phil Jackson's competitive fires. An upset loss to Riley's Heat late in the 1996 season had prompted Jackson to enter the locker room and tell his players, "Never lose to that guy."

Showdown of Styles

So the 1997 Eastern Conference finals became a showdown of coaching styles, Jackson's cerebral approach versus Riley's intensity, Chicago's triangle offense against Miami's clutching, snakebiting, overplaying defense. In other circumstances it might have been the setting for high drama, but the Bulls had always had the Heat figured out. In the 1996 first round, Jackson's troops had swept Miami convincingly, simply by taking away center Alonzo Mourning's pet moves. The Bulls reason for pause this time around had to do with Miami's dramatic improvement. The Heat had won sixty-one games, mainly because point guard Tim Hardaway, in his second season playing for Riley, had gotten comfortable in his surroundings and turned in an All-Star year. Mourning, too, had worked hard at his game and gotten much better over the course of a year.

In most regards, however, Hardaway was the biggest concern. He was the third-straight, high-quality point guard the Bulls would have to face in the postseason. "Tim Hardaway's definitely different from the point guards we've seen," Chicago's Randy Brown said. "He's an exceptional three-point shooter, a great ball handler, a great passer. We just want to pressure him early and make him make difficult plays. Try to make him do things he's not normally used to doing." Those defensive notions worked exceptionally well in Game 1 at the United Center.

As usual, the Bulls took a couple of quarters to read the situation and get untracked. The Heat led 49-38 at the half, which only set up Chicago's trademark third-quarter run, a 21-9 surge that gave the Bulls a one-point edge. The Heat, though, kept their poise and had actually regained the upper hand, 66-61, as the fourth quarter opened. They even managed to hold onto a four-point edge until the five-minute mark when Pippen and Harper hit back-to-back treys that opened the way for Chicago. From there, the Bulls mustered a 7-0 push down the stretch to finish it off, 84-77.

Huge in the edge was Rodman's rebounding presence. He finished with a postseason high nineteen to give Chicago a 54-35 advantage on the boards, which in turn kept Miami from getting out and running to easy baskets. Lacking that opportunity, the Heat was mostly a jump-shooting team, which meant the Bulls forced them to that option, then pressured them into faltering.

"The thing that shocked me the most is just the way we got taken apart at the end," said veteran Heat reserve Ed Pinckney. "The Bulls are able to pressure on all the trigger points of your offense. Next thing you know, the shot clock is down and you're throwin' up a shot from thirty feet out, or you commit a charge or something. It's like a blitz defense."

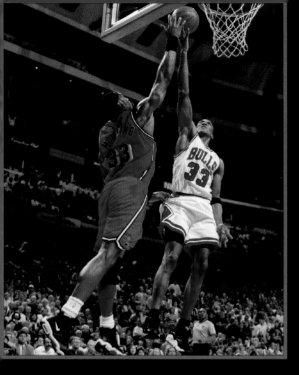

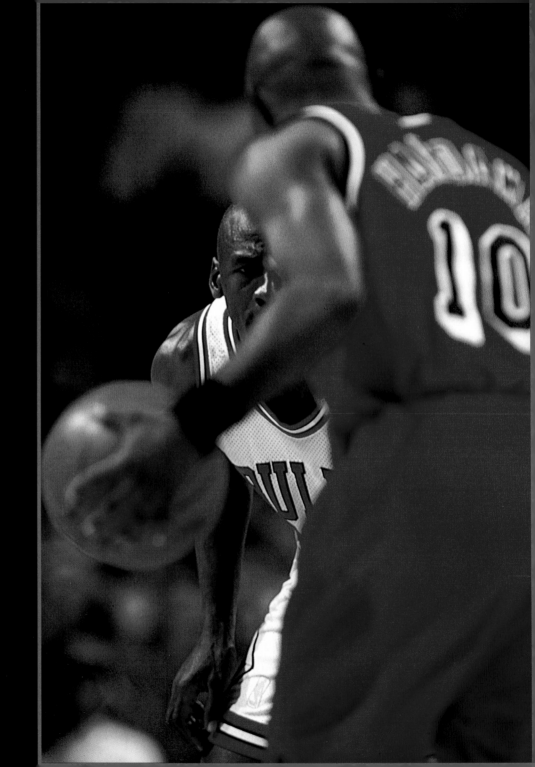

Tex Winter, meanwhile, was merely amazed that "we can continue to win ball games shooting the ball as poorly as we're shooting it right now. Maybe we're forcing some things. They play tough defense, their hands in your face." The most irritating thing about the Heat defense, the Bulls assistant added, was their capacity for getting away with snakebiting, or hitting the shooter on the elbow just enough to knock off his shot. "They're after your elbow," Winter said.

Actually, neither team had managed to shoot the ball well in the atmosphere of frenzied defense, set in motion by Riley's brand of scrambling, holding, bumping, brushing, or anything else that worked. The pattern held true for Game 2, after which Phil Jackson said he could only talk about defense because there was little offense. In fact, the final score for Game 2, a 75-68 Bulls win, set an all-time NBA playoff record low for scoring. Not since the days before the twenty-four-second shot clock was installed had teams turned in such meager totals.

Hardaway, Miami's main weapon, was just five for sixteen from the field. And Jordan made only four of fifteen attempts. "Both teams were frustrated with their offensive play," Jackson said, Miami, a team that specialized in three-point shooting, shot three for twenty-six from beyond the arc.

"It's difficult," Riley said when asked what he could do to free up Hardaway.

One solution to free up his offense from the Bulls' defense, he said, was to get out and run—hard to do against the Bulls. One strategy was to go with a smaller lineup with Mashburn at power forward. One more shooter on the floor stretched out the defense more.

"We played ugly against Atlanta. We played ugly against Washington. It isn't the competition. It's just us. Except for our defense. Our defense has won games," Jordan, whose twenty-three points included fifteen free throws, told reporters afterward. "Our offense has kept people in the stands.

Defense has been winning championships for us in the past." Jordan acknowledged that both he and Pippen had turned in a terrible offensive game. We can look in the mirror and say when we play bad.

The Heat was certainly hoping that trend would continue in Miami. Asked his team's best hope for Game 3, Hardaway replied, "Make it hard for Jordan, make it hard for Scottie. Rebound defensively and run."

So Much for Offense

So how hard was it for Tex Winter, perhaps the game's premier offensive mind, to sit and watch his team get caught up in the lowest-scoring playoff game in league history? "It doesn't bother me so much," he said gamely afterward. "Defense is a factor. The referees are letting a whole lot of contact go, and you don't really get free looks at the basket. They're just into you on every shot; they get their hand in your face. If Riley has a player out there who doesn't have a hand in your face, he's either coming out of the ball game or getting fined or something. And we attempt to do the same thing."

All he would admit was that he was not satisfied with the execution of the offense, the ball movement. But behind the scenes, the wheels were turning for Jackson, Winter, and the rest of the Bulls coaching staff. They hated the kind of ball they were forced to play against Riley's teams. The Bulls bench, their groomed offensive unit, had been outscored 42-16 in the first two games. Something had to change to open up the offense. The Bulls knew that in Miami, the Heat defense would be more clutching than ever, and their three-point shots would be falling.

Something had to be done. So the Chicago coaches spent hours reviewing the tapes of the first two games and came up with a plan to spread their triangle offense, an adjustment they had rarely used over the years. To say the least, it caught Riley and his players flat-footed and opened the back-door lanes to the basket for an array of layups and slams. Both teams opened slowly in the first period, but then the Bulls exploded with a 13-4 run to open the second quarter. To that, they then added another 11-0 run midway through the third, started by three Jordan scores—a dunk, a chip-shot jumper, and a swooping layup. Miami's answer was a turnover on each of four possessions.

The Miami crowd sat miserably, with only Rodman's new dye job—he shifted from his fundamental blond to another wacked-out, multihued look—and dark purple fingernails to keep them entertained as the Bulls smoked their way to the finish, 98-74. What made it so sweet for the Chicago coaching staff were the facts that: 1. It had come against Riley's club; and 2. In a postseason when they had to increasingly rely upon Jordan's one-on-one skills, the offense had delivered in a big way in a crucial game.

Winter, in his understated way, was ecstatic. "We went to an open court a lot more, and I think that that sort of tricked 'em a little bit," he said. "We got a lot of back-cut baskets. It really broke it open for us."

"It was a great coaching move by Phil," observed Jud Buechler, who scored six points in ten minutes of playing time, "because these guys had done such a great job taking us out of our triangle offense, putting a lot of pressure on the wing-entry pass, putting a lot of pressure on all of our passes. What happens is that the inside had become just a big, crowded area. When we opened up the offense, we got those back-cuts, which is what you have to do because they're pressuring the ball and overplaying on the wings. A lot of good things happened out of that."

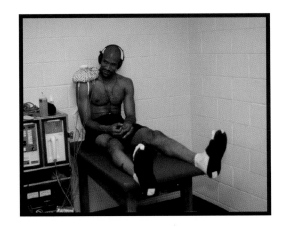

Never one to make excuses, Riley readily acknowledged that he had been outfoxed. "They did something different in their offense today," the Miami coach said. "Instead of going straight to their triangle stuff, they really spread the floor well and made harder cuts. They probably got more layups and reverses and back doors against us today than they've gotten all season."

It was as well as the triangle offense had ever functioned against an aggressive defense, Winter said, adding quickly that the Bulls previous

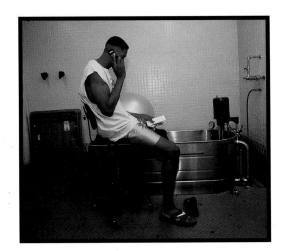

championship teams, featuring John Paxson and Bill Cartwright, probably executed the offense better than the current group. Against many defenses during the regular season, the Bulls are allowed to proceed with their offense with relative freedom. "Sometimes it's kinda like running a skull practice against some of these teams' defenses," Winter said. "It's a beauty to behold. You have a better opportunity because they're giving you more freedom."

Jordan the Team Player

For years, the impression around Chicago was that Jordan had put up a massive resistance to Winter's innovations when Jackson first decided to make them the Bulls primary offense after he took over as head coach in 1989. "He's always been willing," Winter said of Jordan. "The first year he was a little reluctant. But he recognized that if we were going to win championships, we had to do it as a team. He wasn't going to do it as an individual. As you know, Michael had been nurtured in a school of basketball at North Carolina with Dean Smith," Winter added. "In a lot of ways, Michael has been nurtured in this type of team offense concept. Michael is also the kind of guy who has always had a great deal of respect for the title of coach. That doesn't mean he's gonna accept the coach unless the coach wins his respect. Phil Jackson has certainly done that, and this system has proved to be very effective for him. Anytime you win over your superstar the way we've been able to win over Michael, then you've got a very good chance to succeed."

They had done just that in a big way against the Heat. "They're quick, they know what we like to do for our two key players," Riley said of the Bulls defense. "They load up on both 'Zo and Tim; we gotta get other people to step up. But you cannot make a lot of passes against that team. You just can't. You gotta be able to execute with your quality people, and they gotta be able to make plays. 'Zo is a postup player, but they're not allowing him to catch the ball where he wants to catch it. They're shooting two and three guys and stunting at him a lot. With Tim, they're just committed to not letting him do anything. Whatever we tried to do today was simply taken away.

"It's almost like an amoeba defense," Riley said. "They take away angles. They deny your trigger passes. They're long. They switch on everything. They are an exceptional defensive team. You can't rely on just scoring in your half-court. If you're not running and rebounding and getting second shots at every opportunity you get, then it's gonna be very difficult to score."

Both the Bulls coaches and players knew that the Heat would try to push the tempo for Game 4 because running was the only way to get some easy baskets against that amoeba defense. Plus the Bulls knew the Heat would lash back hard to keep from getting swept. At the close of his comments after Game 3, Mourning had even guaranteed that his team would not lose the next game.

It seemed foolhardy at the time, but who could have known that Michael Jordan would decide to play forty-five holes of golf on his day off between games? Who would have figured His Airness to make just two of his first twenty-two shots in Game 4? About the only thing you could count on with Jordan was that no matter how deep a hole he dug for himself and his teammates, he would find a way to bring them rushing back at the end. Finding themselves down twenty-one points with the clock eating away the second half, the Bulls abandoned the triangle offense that had worked so well just the day before and watched Jordan go into his attack mode.

Jordan spurred Chicago on a 22-5 run that pulled the Bulls within four, 61-57, at the end of the third. The Heat surged right back at the beginning of the fourth, pushing their margin back to a dozen, 72-60. Jordan then scored eighteen straight points for Chicago, a display that trimmed the Miami lead

to just one with only 2:19 to go. The ending, however, came down to the Heat making a final six free throws, good enough for a Miami win.

Jordan had scored twenty of Chicago's twenty-three points in the fourth quarter. "When he started making them, they just came, came, came, came, came," said Tim Hardaway. "He's a scorer; he's the man."

Asked about his miserable first half, Jordan glowered, "We're not concerned," he said. "We know we can play better. We showed in the second half the intensity we can play at and how they can get rattled. We feel confident that if we play our game, as we did in the second half, we'll be all right."

They were, of course. The good news in Game 4 was another outstanding effort from Rodman, who finished with thirteen points and eleven rebounds, a performance he would nearly equal back in Chicago in Game 5 with another thirteen rebounds and nine more points.

Jordan, too, continued on his tear from the end of Game 4. He opened Game 5 with fifteen in the first quarter, good enough for a 33-19 Bulls lead and little doubt as to the outcome. The only cloud as they closed out the Heat, 100-87, was a first-quarter foot injury to Pippen that kept him on the bench the last three quarters. On this night, he wasn't needed.

"They are the greatest team since the Celtics won eleven in thirteen years" (from 1957-69), Riley told reporters afterward. "I don't think anybody's going to win again until Michael retires. Sometimes you can build a great team, and you'll never win a championship because you had the misfortune of being born the same time that Jordan went through his run."

Meanwhile, a time zone away, the Houston Rockets and Utah Jazz were battling for the Western Conference title. That, too, seemed of little consequence to Riley. "I think Chicago's going to win it against anybody," he said.

Even before the Eastern Conference finals had concluded, Tex Winter settled in for a late-night television peek at the Western Conference showdown between the Houston Rockets and Utah Jazz. He didn't have to watch long to conclude that from a matchup standpoint, the Bulls would have an easier time in the championship series against the Utah Jazz.

Winter figured that the Rockets' Hakeem Olajuwon and Charles Barkley would make things tough for the Bulls. "Houston just tries to overpower you with Olajuwon or Barkley in the offensive post," he said. "Houston is very difficult for us to match up against."

Regardless, some of the Bulls coaches and players still indicated they would prefer to meet Houston in the Finals. After all, the Rockets were the "other" team of the 1990s, having won the league title in '94 and '95 when Jordan left the NBA to try his hand at minor league baseball. Beating Houston for the championship would clearly establish that the Bulls owned the decade.

Utah's John Stockton, however, settled the issue in Game 6 of the Western Conference finals with a last-second shot that sent the Jazz to the league championship series for the first time in their three decades of existence. It was an outcome that didn't displease Winter. "I like the way Utah plays," the Bulls offensive coordinator said. "They're effective, and they have a system. They're a lot like us. They've been together a long time. They stay within the framework of their system."

There was another emotional reason for Chicago fans to greet Utah in the Finals. For almost a decade, Jazz coach Jerry Sloan had been "Mr. Chicago Bull" during his playing days in the Windy City, leading the

Bulls with his hard-nosed, physical style of play. He had even served as an assistant and later the team's head coach, right up until his firing in 1981. Sloan, of course, brushed aside any sentiment about his old Chicago connections in the championship matchup. And the Bulls did the same.

To get his players ready for the championship round, Phil Jackson brought yet another movie out of the dustbin, *Silverado*, a 1985 Western starring Kevin Kline, Kevin Costner, and Danny Glover, a selection obscure enough to test even the memory of film critic and rabid Bulls fan Gene Siskel.

Silverado? Standing courtside before a Finals game, Siskel admitted he'd have to go to the office to get some old notes before he could recall much about it. *Silverado*, a Lawrence Kasdan shoot-'em-up featuring four good outlaws who take on the bad sheriff in a western town, left the coaching staff as puzzled as the players. "Phil doesn't discuss these things with us," assistant Jimmy Rodgers said of Jackson's film choices. "He doesn't say 'I'm going to do *Silverado* for these reasons.' The coaching staff— we follow it along with everyone else, trying to figure out, exactly what messages are we relaying here? I think there's a little bit of mystery involved in all of this. I see some things involved in *Silverado*, where, yes, it's a wild western type of format. But I see a group of guys coming together who have to take care of business."

"He plays the whole movie," Wennington said of Jackson. "He shows two or three minutes at a time. Then he shows game clips and game film—then another two or three minutes of the movie again. He alternates back and forth and eventually (over the course of a playoff series) you see the whole

movie. At different times he'll stress different things. If something happens on the floor, if a player did something bad or something, there'll be a part of the movie that we see that stresses that."

Early each morning after a game, the Bulls coaching staff would dig into the videotape of the night before, breaking down the action frame-by-frame because Jackson wanted his staff to understand fully what had happened. "We want to fully evaluate what we did well, and what we didn't do," Rodgers said. "Then we stress it in the next practice."

The humor of the feature films helped not only the coaches but also the players deal with the boredom of breaking down games frame by frame. "It's almost overwhelming at times," Rodgers said of the amount of videotape the coaching staff and team analyze during a season.

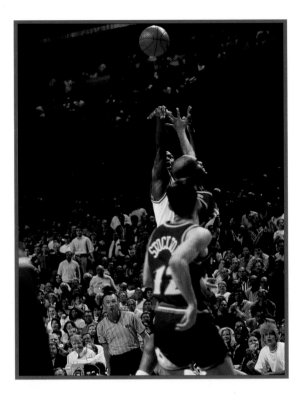

Jackson also seemed amused by the head-scratching that went along with *Silverado*. "I'm enjoying watching the sequences as we go along," Tex Winter admitted. "But as far as any message is concerned, I haven't read anything into it yet. I don't know if the players have or not. It's one of those quick-draw movies, quick-gun movies, and I guess the key to it is that you better react quicker than the opposition." And you certainly better shoot better than they do.

That became eminently clear on Sunday, June 1, in Game 1 of the 1997 NBA Finals, broadcast to a worldwide audience. The comforting sight for Bulls fans was Pippen grinning broadly in pregame warm-ups and playfully taking on teammate Randy Brown in a quick little bout of one-on-one. He hopped around on his feet and seemed very ready to go, despite having suffered the foot injury against Miami.

The other welcome sight for old-time Bulls fans was Jerry Sloan, hands jammed in pockets, awaiting the introductions, scanning the Chicago crowd. The moment he had waited a career for was about to begin. He had virtually cut his heart out to get to the Finals for eight seasons as a player in

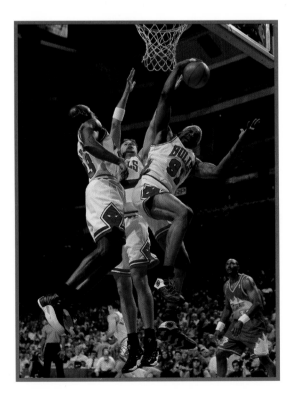

Chicago. In this most delicious of ironies, he had finally reached it, to face his old team, the team that had retired his Number 4. Now it was hanging as a banner at the far west end of the building, one of only two jerseys honored in the United Center rafters, the other being Bob Love's Number 10. Sloan and Love had been teammates on Bulls teams that put together a run of fifty-win seasons in the 1970s and came achingly close to playing their way into the 1975 championship series.

The view of Sloan's banner was largely obscured from his seat on the visitor's bench at the east end of the building, which for Sloan was just as well, because he wanted to put all those old ghosts, all those old Bulls frustrations out of his mind.

It was, however, a night for legends. Muhammad Ali was introduced before tip-off, sporting a colorful leather Bulls jacket, prompting the building to erupt with chants of "*Ali! Ali! Ali!*"

Speaking of heavyweights, Utah's Karl "The Mailman" Malone had been named the league's regular season Most Valuable Player with the announcing of the balloting just a few days earlier. He had narrowly edged Jordan, the prime contender and four-time winner of the award. Jordan said he didn't mind the Jazz power forward getting the individual honor so long as the Bulls claimed the team championship at the end of playoffs. Now the stars and their respective teams were meeting to settle the matter on the court, with fans in both Chicago and Utah eager to seize on the issue, chanting "*MVP!*" when one or the other stepped to the free throw line at key moments throughout the series.

The Jazz rushed out to a solid start in Game 1 by throwing quick double-teams at Jordan and working the boards hard, good enough for a quick Utah lead. Lest the Jazz get too confident, the Luv A Bulls issued a reminder by performing a "We Are The Champions of the World" routine during a time-out.

A Polite Beginning

From its earliest action, the series showed a gentlemanly tone, one not always seen in NBA championship play. When Antoine Carr fouled Randy Brown early in the proceedings, the Utah forward walked over to check on Brown, patted him on the back and helped him up. Yet even the feel-good atmosphere couldn't alleviate the tension, evidenced by Chicago's 40 percent shooting in the first half. Utah was slightly better at 44 percent, with John Stockton scoring eleven and Malone ten. Utah's Bryon Russell hit a three-pointer just before the buzzer to give the Jazz a 42-38 halftime lead.

Jeff Hornacek scored eleven points in the third period to help keep Utah in the lead, except for a brief run by Chicago that netted a one-point edge. The fourth opened with Utah clutching a two-point lead in the face of a mountain of Chicago's trademark pressure.

With just less than eight minutes to go, Stockton hit a jumper, pushing the Utah lead to 70-65, which Harper promptly answered with a trey. Surging on that momentum, the Bulls managed to stay close and even took a one-point edge on a Longley jumper with three minutes left.

Malone responded with two free throws, but Harper snuck inside for an offensive rebound moments later and passed out to Pippen for a trey that put Chicago up, 81-79. For most teams, that would have been enough pressure for a fold, but Stockton hit a three of his own with fifty-five seconds left to make it 82-81, Utah.

Then at the 35.8 mark, Hornacek fouled Jordan, who stepped to the line with the building chanting "*MVP!*" He hit the first to tie it, then missed the second, sending the crowd back to its nervous silence. The Jazz promptly spread the floor and worked the shot clock. As it ran down, Stockton missed a trey, but Rodman fouled Malone on the rebound.

As Malone prepared to shoot his free throws, Pippen whispered in his ear, "The Mailman doesn't deliver on a Sunday." To ensure that, the crowd

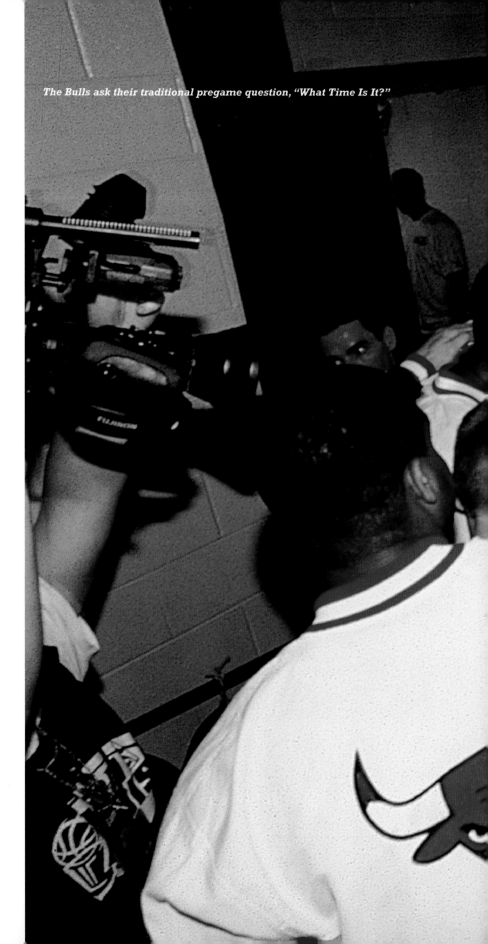

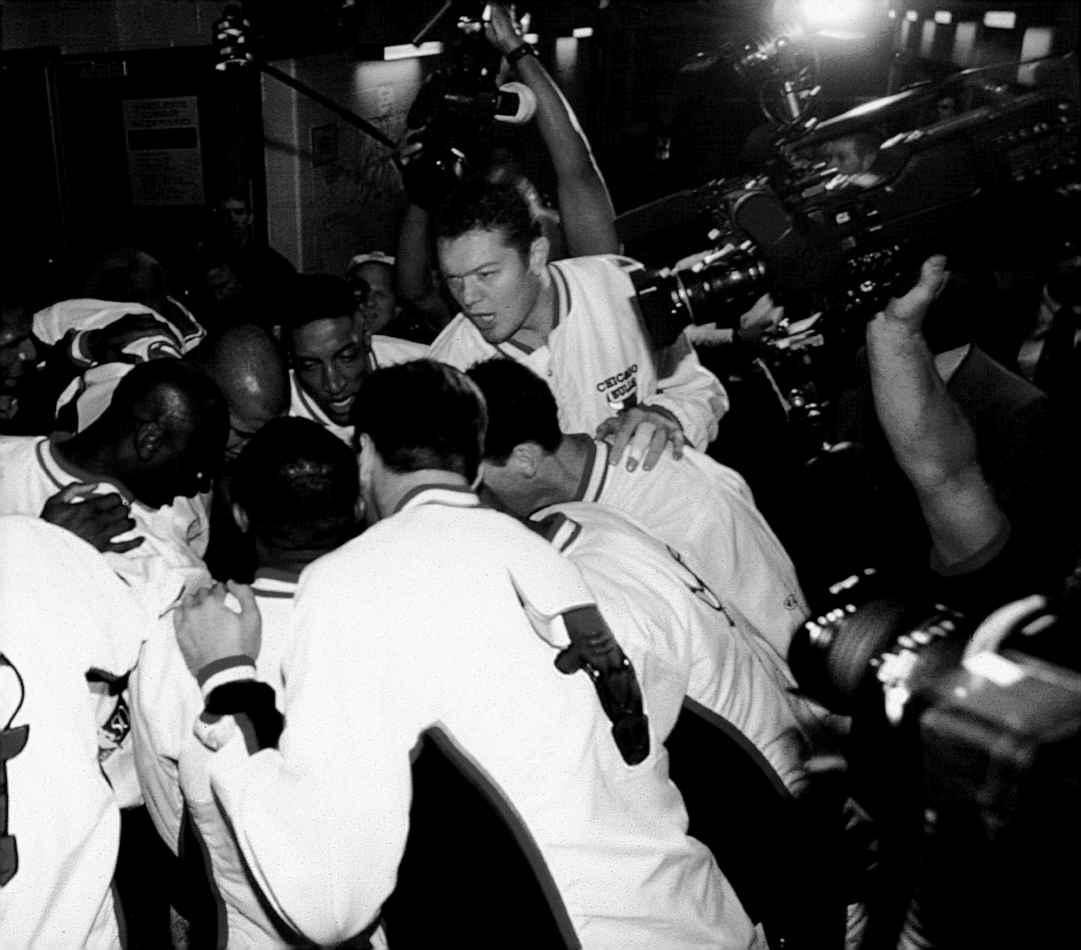

raised a ruckus. His first shot rolled off the rim, and the building exploded in celebration. He stepped back from the line in disgust, then moved back up, wiped his hand on his shirt, dropped eight short dribbles, and missed again, bringing yet another outburst of delight from the crowd as the Bulls controlled the rebound with 7.5 seconds left.

The faces were long in the Jazz huddle during the ensuing time-out. Now they had to defend against Jordan on a buzzer-beater. Amazingly, they decided not to double-team him. Pippen inbounded the ball to Kukoc, who quickly dumped it off to Jordan, who executed a move on Bryon Russell and broke free just inside the three-point line on the left side. The entire building froze there for an instant upon the release of the shot. When it swished, twenty-one thousand fans leaped instantly in exultation, a strange sight of simultaneous overstimulation, almost like something you'd see on the Nature Channel, when the cilia on the underbelly of some sea creature get zapped by the light.

The shot gave the Bulls the win, 84-82, and the Jazz sank instantly, knowing they had just lost any hopes they had of controlling the series. Jordan had finished with thirty-one points on thirteen of twenty-seven shooting while Malone rebounded after missing seven of his first eight shots to score twenty-three on the night with fifteen rebounds.

The unsung hero was Chicago's defense, which forced Utah into a playoff-high eighteen turnovers, including seven from Stockton. The Jazz point guard finished with sixteen points and twelve assists.

One Team Was Loose

The Bulls opened Game 2 three nights later as loose as the Jazz was tight, and the scoring showed it. Jordan hit a jumper, then Pippen finished off a Harper back-door pass with a sweet little reverse, and moments later Longley broke free for an enthusiastic stuff. Like that, the Jazz was in a maze and couldn't find its way out.

Long known for their sadism, the Bulls marketing team set up Part II of Malone's little chamber of personal horrors by declaring it clacker night and passing out noisemakers by the thousands to fans as they entered the building. A similar ploy had completely unnerved Miami's Alonzo Mourning in the first round of the '96 playoffs. Now it was The Mailman's turn.

When Longley fouled Malone ninety seconds into the game, the clackers were waiting and rattled him into two free throw misses. Two minutes later, when Malone went to the line again with the Jazz trailing 8-1, the whole barn was rattling like a giant playpen. This time, Malone stepped up and hit both. Given a momentary rush of confidence, Utah closed to 14-13 at the 4:41 mark of the first period.

Jordan was on fire, though, and quickly quashed any momentum with a trey and a jumper. Then he fed Kerr for a pair of three-pointers, and, like that, Chicago had stretched the lead to 25-15 with 1:30 left in the period, which had twenty-four thousand fans on their feet clapping and pounding to "Wooly Bully." On this night, the fans seemed intent on refuting any allegations of their passivity. They were in it early and often, pleading "*Deee-fense*" even as the Bulls opened a lead.

The Jazz dug in and made a run in the second period, bringing it to 31-29 with a Malone bucket. Just when it seemed Utah might find some life, the killer emerged in Jordan. He drove the Bulls on a tear to a 47-31 lead, scoring and drawing fouls like only he could. At every trip to the free throw line, the fans greeted Jordan with lusty chants of "*MVP! MVP!*"

The third period brought only more frustration for Utah. The Bulls' defensive strategy continued to force Stockton to the baseline, continued

to make even the simple things difficult. When Kukoc hit a three-pointer midway through the period, Chicago had forged ahead 60-40. Yet Jordan was far from through. The Jazz managed to knock the ball away from him in the lane with four minutes left in the third and his team up by twenty-one, and while his teammates headed upcourt to play defense, Jordan dived into the scrum on the floor to get a piece of a loose ball and force a jump ball.

Now it was time to show off (sometimes you wonder if MJ even knows he's doing it). He took a feed from Kukoc on the high right post, quickly circled the defense hard right along the baseline, intent like some shark moving in for the kill, then knifed in at the appropriate moment to cut through an opening for one of his eye-popping reverses, one of those Jordan gymnastic feats with a 9.5 degree of difficulty. Before the fans had even settled back into their seats from cheering, he followed it up with a deep two that pushed the lead to 70-48.

How big was his hunger? That seemed to be the only question. He brought the ball up the floor moments later and paused in the middle of his dribble with his arms thrown wide, calling for a spread floor. He had thirty already, and he wanted more.

Jordan finished the night with thirty-eight points, thirteen rebounds, and nine assists. He would have registered a triple double if Pippen hadn't blown a late layup, costing him the tenth assist. No matter, the Bulls coasted to a 2-0 series lead, 97-85.

"I thought we were intimidated right from the beginning of the game," Sloan said afterward. "If you allow them to destroy your will to win, it's hard to compete—I didn't think we put all our energy into competing tonight."

Caffey gets a look at the Utah canyons out the window of the team bus.

Wennington, the proud owner of a Harley, became buddies with the Utah State Police assigned as the team's escort during the Finals.

The Jazz, the team that led the league in field-goal percentage, had shot just 40 percent from the floor and scored just eleven points in the second period, tying the Bulls' own NBA Finals record low, set in Game 4 of the 1996 series against Seattle.

Around the press room and in the stands, people were complaining that the Finals was headed toward a sweep. But the twisted scowl on Stockton's face said the series was headed to Utah, where he would get his team a win or die trying.

The Meaning of Silverado

By the time the Bulls got to Utah, Bill Wennington had figured out why Phil Jackson chose *Silverado* for his championship series film. It was all about location. "Being out in the prairies," the injured center surmised, "comin' out here, pastures, cows."

If that were the case, perhaps Jackson should have chosen *Breathless*, because the four-thousand-foot altitude in Salt Lake City had the Bulls winded for the better part of a week. The team stayed in the nearby ski resort of Park City, which has an elevation of about eight thousand feet, in hopes it would help the players adjust for game time on Friday, June 6. But the Jazz took a 61-46 halftime lead and did a little coasting of its own, pulling the series to 2-1 with a 104-93 victory, during which Jazz fans showered Malone with MVP chants of their own. He answered their support by scoring thirty-seven points with ten rebounds to lead the rout.

The tone for the Friday night contest was set early with the unleashing of an introduction and prolonged applause perhaps unlike anything seen before in championship series history. A dozen giant bags dumped an avalanche of aqua, gold, white, and purple balloons from the rafters in conjunction with a battery of fireworks blasting away at center court, the result of which made the place sound an awful lot like Beirut, a sensation drawn out over the next several minutes as the fans popped thousands of balloons, like the crackling of small arms fire. At the height of the spectacle, the Jazz mascot rolled a full-throated Harley Davidson motorcycle onto the floor, revving and rumbling and smoking in defiance.

The whole display was way over the top, Phil Jackson later told reporters, an opinion the Bulls coaching staff reinforced by inserting earplugs for the introductions of the next two games.

Yet noise was a minor concern alongside the Bulls' struggling offense. They had managed to scare the Jazz with a 16-3 run in the second half, driven by Jordan's and Pippen's three-point shooting (Pippen even tied an NBA Finals record with seven treys). But the Jazz had found success by bumping Chicago's shooters in the low post and forcing the Bulls to take perimeter shots. The result was the opening of a crease in Chicago's confidence.

Radio Days in Utah

To make sure the Bulls didn't get too comfortable for Sunday's Game 4, a local radio station began attempting early wake-up calls at their quarters, and someone went to the extra effort of having a band strike up an early-morning tune outside the visitors' quarters in Park City, all in response to a similar ploy aimed at the Jazz by a radio station in Chicago earlier in the series.

Jordan's effort was to overlook the distractions by talking about his primary goal, winning a championship ring for new assistant coach Frank Hamblen, who had joined the Bulls prior to the season after many years in

Milwaukee. "I've been talking about it all season long, especially with Ham," Jordan said.

The presumptions of a championship, however, were once again set aside in the din of Utah's Delta Center for Game 4 on Sunday, June 8. Encouraged by Jackson's complaints, Utah's fans and game operations staff were ready with another round of exploding fireworks and thunderous applause, highlighted by some furry creature rappelling out of the rafters with spinning sparklers exploding on its head. Fortunately, the only motorcycle on the premises this time was Malone's, and it was parked in a storage area.

Regardless, the afternoon unfolded as what was easily the Bulls' biggest disappointment of the season. Their offense still sputtered, but their defense for forty-five minutes was spectacular. In short, they played well enough to win, and should have. With 2:38 to go in the game, they had willed their way to a 71-66 lead and seemed set to control the series 3-1. But that's when John Stockton took over with a series of plays, and the Bulls uncharacteristically stumbled.

Stockton immediately reversed the momentum with a twenty-five-foot three-pointer. Jordan came right back with a trey, and when Hornacek missed a runner, the Bulls had a chance to close it out. Instead, Stockton timed a steal from Jordan at the top of the key and drove the length of the court. In a move that awed Sloan, Jordan recovered, raced downcourt, and managed to block the shot, only to get whistled for a body foul, a call that might not have been made in Chicago, Jordan later pointed out.

Stockton made one of two to pull Utah within three. Pippen then missed a corner jumper, Stockton was fouled and made both with 1:03 left to cut the lead back to 73-72. Jordan missed a jumper on the next possession, Stockton rebounded and looped a perfect, long pass down to Malone for a 74-73 Utah lead.

"If you could have suspended time while the ball was in the air, Jerry would have strangled me," Stockton said of Sloan's courtside agony over his daring pass.

The Bulls' next possession brought a wide-open Steve Kerr a three-pointer from the right corner that missed. With seventeen seconds left, Chicago fouled Malone, setting up repeat circumstances from Game 1. Would he miss again in the clutch? Pippen wanted to talk to him about that, but Hornacek stepped in to keep him away from The Mailman. "I knew what he was doing, trying to talk to me," Malone said. "He still talked to me the whole time I was shooting."

His first shot knocked around the rim before falling in, smoothing the way for the second and a 76-73 lead. With no time-outs, the Bulls were left with only a rushed three-point miss by Jordan, which Utah punctuated with a breakaway slam for the 78-73 final, the second lowest scoring game in league championship history. The Series was deadlocked at 2-2.

An Agonizing Wait

After moving at a breakneck pace, playing every other day, the NBA Finals slowed down again, giving the Bulls an agonizing three-day wait before pivotal Game 5 on Wednesday. Asked about the time off, an obviously despondent Steve Kerr said, "I try not to think about it. It hasn't been fun."

Rodman, in particular, was restless. He had played well defensively the first two games of the series, but his performances during the two losses had Tex Winter worried that the energetic forward had been intimidated by the officials. Rodman's answer to the anxiety was to ask Phil Jackson's permission for a jet ride to Las Vegas for some overnight gambling after Sunday's loss. "It's no big deal," Rodman said upon his return. "I was just enjoying myself, trying to get ready for the game."

Asked about Rodman's getaway, Jordan pointed out the Bulls were "mentally and physically exhausted. If that's his way of getting away and getting a renewed attitude, I don't have a problem with it—as long as he comes back ready to play Wednesday."

A dehydrated Jordan has his blood pressure and vitals checked by team doctor Jeffrey Weinberg after Game 1.

Actually none of the Bulls seemed too relaxed. Kukoc was shooting 34 percent for the series and averaging 7.5 points. Kerr had made only three of his twelve trey attempts. Harper was shooting 33 percent and averaging 5.5 points. Rodman was averaging a little over five rebounds in each of the first four games. Even Jordan, who had shot 51 percent in the first two games, had seen his shooting drop to 40 percent in the next two.

The anxiety was hanging over the Bulls like the thunderstorms that rolled up Utah's cottonwood canyons as Game 5 approached. Just when it seemed their predicament couldn't get worse, Jordan was hit with a viral illness in the wee hours before Wednesday's game. The first shock of the news hit his teammates at the morning pregame shoot-around. He was too sick to attend. Jordan miss a practice? *Never!*

The stillness that settled over the team in the hours before Game 5 unsettled second-year forward Jason Caffey. ''It's kinda scary,'' he said, sitting wide-eyed in the locker room before the game. ''You don't know what's going on when it's like this.'' Never had a Bulls locker room been so quiet.

About the only sound in the room was equipment man John Ligmanowski whistling as he worked, trying to cut the tension. In the darkness of the training room a few feet away, Jordan lay like some sick puppy. However, some veteran Bulls observers weren't fooled. ''Michael's sick?'' one asked. ''He'll score forty.''

Actually the total came to thirty-eight, including the back-breaking three down the stretch to deliver the Bulls from the dizzying altitude. Despite his well-known flair for the dramatic, this performance was no act. ''I've played a lot of seasons with Michael, and I've never seen him so sick,'' Pippen said afterward. ''I didn't know if he would even put his uniform on. He's the greatest and definitely the MVP in my mind.''

The Jazz came out strong, riding on the emotion of their crowd and the confidence of their twenty-three-game home winning streak. Jordan scored Chicago's first four points, then faltered weakly while Utah rushed out to a sixteen-point lead early in the second quarter, 34-18 on an Antoine Carr jumper.

Jordan, though, fixed his focus on the rim and started taking the ball inside. He contributed six points on a 19-6 Chicago run that pulled the Bulls to 42-39. Malone, meanwhile, was forced to sit with an early third foul. Jordan's inside work also produced eight free throws in the quarter and helped give Chicago its first lead, 45-44. Malone again found more foul trouble in the third as the pace slowed, but Utah forged a five-point lead to start the fourth and expanded it to eight early in the quarter.

But it was Michael Time. He scored fifteen points down the stretch to shove the pressure right at the Jazz. The Bulls were down by one when he went to the free throw line with forty-six seconds to go. He hit the first but snatched up the loose ball when he missed the second. Moments later he hit a three on a pass from Pippen, pushing the Bulls to an 88-85 lead.

Utah's Greg Ostertag scored on a dunk to cut Chicago's lead to 88-87 with fifteen seconds left. But on the ensuing inbounds play, Pippen dribbled into the open court and found Longley underneath for a slam. Up 90-87, the Bulls relied on their defense to force Hornacek into an off-balance three-pointer. The Jazz controlled the miss, and Stockton made a final free throw. But the Bulls had ridden their championship experience to a decisive 3-2 series lead. Jordan stood under the Utah basket jutting his fists into the air triumphantly as the game ended.

"As far as big wins, I think this is as big a win as we've had in a playoff situation like this, especially getting down in the first half and having fought

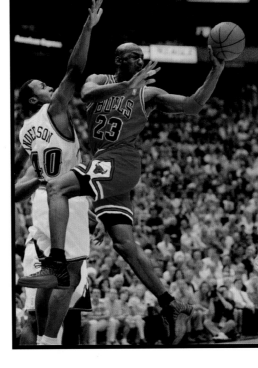

back," Phil Jackson said. "I almost played myself into passing out," Jordan said. "I came in and I was dehydrated, and it was all to win a basketball game. I gave a lot of effort, and I'm just glad we won because it would have been devastating if we had lost. I was really tired, very weak at halftime. I told Phil to use me in spurts, but somehow I found the energy to stay strong, and I wanted it really bad."

He had hit thirteen for twenty-seven from the field with seven rebounds, five assists, three steals, and a block. "He hadn't gotten out of bed all day, standing up was literally a nauseating experience, and he had dizzy spells and so forth," Jackson said. "We were worried about his amount of minutes, but he said, 'Let me play,' and he played forty-four minutes. That's an amazing effort in itself."

Pippen had seventeen points, ten rebounds, and five assists, but there were no statistics to describe his defensive play. "Michael was great, this we all know," said Houston's Charles Barkley, who was sitting courtside in the Delta Center. "But I thought one of the keys to the game was the second quarter. Utah had a chance to blow the Bulls out and didn't. One of the reasons the Jazz didn't was because Scottie made some big plays during Chicago's run."

A Happy Ending

The series finally returned to Chicago and on the morning of Game 6, the players begged Phil Jackson not to make them watch more basketball video clips. "Let's just watch the end of *Silverado*," they said. In the film, the group of good guys had become fragmented only to come

together at the end for a glorious shoot-out with the bad guys. Sensing the mood had built just right, Jackson agreed to run the tape through to the end.

Togetherness, of course, was the clear and perfect answer to the predicament. Jordan finished the season's business that night, of course. A perfect Hollywood ending. The Jazz valiantly took the lead early and kept it until the Bulls pressure finally ate it away down the stretch, with Jordan driving home the issue. Thirty-nine more points and two hours of defense, all capped off with the sweetest little assist to Steve Kerr, the same Steve Kerr who had been groaning in his sleep and talking to himself because he had missed a wide-open three that could have sent Game 4 into overtime, the kind of miss that had them fussin' back in Downers Grove that "Pax woulda made it."

"Steve's been fighting with himself because of Game 4," Michael explained afterward. "He missed a three-pointer, and he went back to his room. He doesn't know this. His wife told me he was very frustrated. He kept his head in the pillow for hours because he let the team down, because everyone knows he's probably one of the best shooters in the game, and he had the opportunity to pick us up and give us a lift, and he was very disappointed."

Always looking to use everything, Jordan knew that the desire for absolution would run strong at the end of Game 6. "When Phil drew up the play at the end, which everybody in the gym, everybody on TV knew was coming to me, I looked at Steve and said, 'This is your chance, because I know

(Utah's John) Stockton is going to come over and help. And I'm going to come to you.' And he said, 'Give me the ball.' "

The response struck Jordan as something that John Paxson would have said. And we all know how much Jordan respected Paxson and his ability to knock down that open shot, just as we know how Jordan and Kerr clashed after Michael returned to the team in 1995.

"Tonight Steve Kerr earned his wings from my perspective," Jordan said, "because I had faith in him, and I passed him the ball, and he knocked down the shot. I'm glad he redeemed himself, because if he'd have missed that shot, I don't think he could have slept all summer long. I'm very happy for Steve Kerr."

It was a brilliant, sweet, delicious cameo, one that Chicago will treasure. But the show remains Michael's because NBA championships ultimately are always a test of will, and for the 1997 title, he produced the ultimate display of it, in sickness and in health.

"It's been a fight," he admitted afterward. "It's all guts, deep-down determination, what your motives are, what your ambitions were from the beginning. There's been a lot of soul-searching. It's easy to sit back and say, 'I've given my best, I'm tired. Somebody else has got to do it.' Or whatever. I didn't take that approach. I thought positive and did whatever I could do. Every little inch of energy that I have I'm going to provide for this team."

Jordan's true companion throughout the playoffs, while much of the rest of the roster struggled, was Scottie Pippen, who played off Jordan masterfully.

Michael was the obvious series MVP, but Pippen was there throughout, so much so that Jordan said he would keep the MVP trophy but give Scottie the car that accompanies the award.

"I'm going to make sure he gets the car," Michael said, "because he's like a little brother to me." Actually, there was no car given with the award in 1997. For Pippen, that didn't matter. He had Jordan's friendship and respect. In the "Breakfast Club," Ron Harper, Jordan, and Pippen had worked out together each morning. It was the conditioning that delivered a championship.

"He goes through the pain, and we work out every day," Jordan said of Pippen. "He's joining me, working out every day to stay healthy and get out here and provide for the organization and the city so that we can be healthy and continue to be champions."

Pippen the accomplice. Jordan the master.

Ultimately, the only thing that could bring this team together was the relentless, undying effort of Michael Jordan, from the very first tip-off of this uneven season right down to the downpour of red streamers and red, white, and blue confetti in the United Center as the place collapsed into celebration. The alpha and omega of everything was Jordan's performances, one after another, each so brilliant that picking a best is nearly impossible.

Asked earlier in the playoffs to discuss one of Jordan's magical moments, Steve Kerr had smiled and said, "I can't talk about Michael Jordan. I'm not even on the same planet he is."

Finally, in Game 6 of the 1997 NBA Finals, for the sweetest, slightest, most significant instant, Kerr inhabited Michael's planet. In fact, we all did. Thank goodness for that.

The team prayer after their Game 6 victory in Chicago.

...ippen spoke with President Clinton after the victory.

Rodman told the crowd at Grant Park during the championship celebration, "I'll be back, baby."

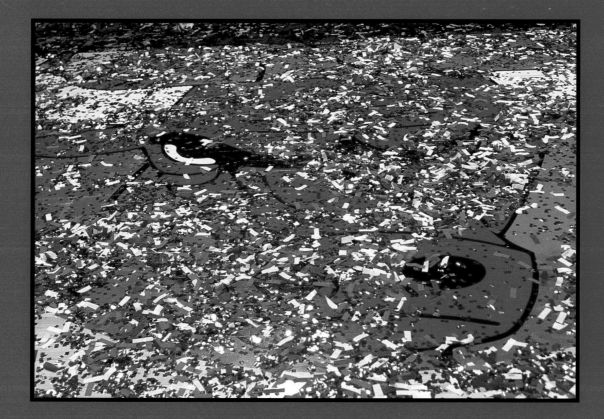